Virginia County Records

VOLUME IX

EDITED BY

William Armstrong Crozier

CLEARFIELD

Originally Published As
Virginia County Records
Volume IX
The Genealogical Association
Hasbrouck Heights, New Jersey, 1911

Reprinted
Genealogical Publishing Co., Inc.
Baltimore, Maryland
1971

Reprinted for
Clearfield Company, Inc. by
Genealogical Publishing Co., Inc.
Baltimore, Maryland
1993, 1997, 2001

Library of Congress Catalogue Card Number 67-29835
International Standard Book Number: 0-8063-0472-3

Made in the United States of America

The publisher gratefully acknowledges
the loan of the original of this book
by the
Virginia State Library
Richmond, Virginia

Vol. IX   MARCH 1911   Part I

Virginia County Records

PUBLISHED QUARTERLY

EDITED BY

William Armstrong Crozier, F. R. S., F. G. S. A.

Published by
The Genealogical Association
Hasbrouck Heights
New Jersey

FIVE DOLLARS A YEAR

Virginia County Records

Published Quarterly

CONTENTS OF PART I

Virginia County Records

QUARTERLY MAGAZINE

| VOL. IX | MARCH 1911 | No. 1 |

INDEX TO LAND GRANTS

RAPPAHANNOCK COUNTY.

(Continued from Vol. VI.)

Book No. 6.

Page	Name	Date	No. acres
217	Wm. Mathew	1668	1148
226	Thos. Pattison	1669	1626
226	John Pate	1669	1200
231	Thos. Edmondson	1667	220
245	Henry Awberry	1669	480
542	Lt. Col. Thos. Goodrich	1669	2876
254	Lt. Col. Thos. Goodrich	1659	1800
255	Wm. White	1667	150
269	Bickett Burke	1669	408
276	Thos. Wright and John Chynn	1670	220
282	Edward Reyley and John Killingham	1670	500
286	Warwick Cammock	1670	1923
286	John Meader	1670	625
286	Robert Beverley	1670	2000
291	Thos. Parker	1669	120
291	Wm. Lane	1669	1438
291	Rich'd Holt	1669	600
292	Wm. Bruse	1669	250
293	Luke Billington	1669	679
293	Henry Clarke	1669	1495
295	Capt. John Hull	1669	650

RICHMOND COUNTY.

BOOK No. 1.

BOOK No. 2.

41	James Story	1704	441
49	Capt. John Tarpley	1704	100
64	Lewis Griffie	1704	414
65	Robert Clerk	1704	1954
67	John Hanxford	1704	100
70	Sem. Cox and Wm. Berry	1704	349
78	Wm. Smoot	1704	409
79	John and James Indgoe	1704	307
80	Abraham Goad	1704	208
81	Richard Fowler	1704	230
87	Joseph Belfield	1704	555
95	John Turberville	1705	798
96	Hancock Lee	1705	1100
100	John Hanxford	1705	77
101	Hancock Lee	1705	470
103	Wm. Combs	1705	100
109	John Symons	1705	130
107	James Innis	1705	104
111	Wm. Combs	1705	100
114	Thomas Pannell	1705	135
116	James Storey	1705	32
117	Capt. John Tarpley	1705	180
122	John Smith	1705	392
123	Wm. Stewart	1705	133½
128	Wm. Wood	1705	500
134	Wm. Pannell	1706	45
135	Thomas Rout	1706	120
144	Henry Long	1706	162
148	Capt. Wm. Ball	1706	1093
156	Peter Ellis	1706	118
157	John and Augustine Higgins	1706	110
159	James Thomas	1707	729
162	Thomas Paise	1707	320
167	Thomas Tibbet	1707	37
172	Maj. William Robinson	1707	3036
181	Thomas Griffin	1707	3471
183	George Glasscock	1707	44½
202	Capt. Charles Barber	1708	85

203	John Loyd	1708	384½
206	Capt. Wm. Barber	1708	80
207	Thomas White	1708	51
208	George Greer	1708	885
209	John Burkett and Wm. Pannell	1708	300
210	Robert Harrison	1708	218
213	Andrew Dew	1708	302
218	Charles Carter	1709	350
219	Philip Ludwell	1709	2020
221	Same	1709	3840
224	Ed. Mountjoy and Thomas Brooks	1709	800
229	James Coward	1709	121
230	Wm. Brown	1709	38
232	Henry Gallop	1709	109
233	James Innis	1709	333
238	Thomas Bryan	1709	166½
255	Charles Carter	1709	1100
258	Same	1709	242
257	Same	1709	77
259	Richard Buckner	1709	20
263	Maurice Clark	1710	150

Book No. 4.

5	Wm. Allen and John Brown	1710	713
11	Francis Stern	1710	50
12	Benjamin Berryman	1710	200
13	Same	1710	100
14	Same	1710	100
19	Henry Bruse	1710	274
21	John Brown and Wm. Allen	1710	427
25	Raleigh Downman	1710	30½
35	Mark Tune	1711	289
38	Andrew Dew	1711	78
41	John Hartley	1711	153
46	Edward Barrow	1711	50
47	Wm. Page	1711	436
67	Edward Fagan	1712	150
68	John Tarpley	1712	50 A. 91 Per.

BOOK No. 5.

75 James Key 1715   2180
76 Thomas Glasscock ....1715 70A. 70 Per.
80 James Warren 1715   168

CAROLINE COUNTY MARRIAGE BONDS.

(Continued from Vol. VII.)

The following ministers are mentioned in the records as
having performed the marriages given:, John Young, John
Sorrell, Theodorick Noele, Henry Goodloe, John Self,
Thomas Mastin, Archer Moody, and Abner Waugh.

Sept.	28, 1794.	Isaac Seysil and Betty Page Dillard.
Jan.	11, 1793.	Alex. Sneed and Sukey Sneed.
Jan.	14, 1796.	Sam Schooler and Anne Williams.
Feb.	26, 1796.	Henry Stuart and Betsy Richeson.
Sept.	30, 1797.	Samuel Sneed and Polly Daniel.
Feb.	25, 1799.	James Samuel and Betsy Samuel.
———,	1798.	John Self and Aggy Bowler
Oct.	9, 1795.	Thornton Seal and Molly Bell.
Dec.	22, 1796.	Francis Self and Sally Bolware.
———,	1797.	Gabriel Slaughter and Sally Hord.
Oct.	19, 1797.	Thomas Southworth and Betty Barlow.
April	18, 1787.	———— Thurston and Caty Reynolds.
April	30, 1789.	Wm. Tinsley and Dolly Estis.
Oct.	31, 1789.	Edward Thacker and Priscilla Yarbrough.
———,	1790.	John Turner and Fanny Davis.
———,	1792.	Wm. Taylor and Barbara Allen.
Mar.	24, 1794.	Bartholomew Taylor and Frances Loving.
Sept.	17, 1794.	William Tignor and Frances Covinton.
June	14, 1796.	John Tranham and Mary Daniel.
Feb.	26, 1797.	Lewis Tarrant and Elizabeth Redd.
May	3, 1797.	Wilson Turner and Polly Hurt.
July	28, 1799.	George Tiller and Lucy Mills.
Dec.	26, 1798.	Christopher Terrell and Mary Collins.
Dec.	28, 1798.	Daniel Tiller and Rebecca Camall.
Sept.	6, 1798.	Allen Thomas and Eliza Fowler.
Jan.	12, 1798.	William Tucker and Margaret Scanland.
Sept.	27, 1799.	Godfrey Toler and Charity Barnes.

Dec. 11, 1799. John Trainham and Fanny Richeson.
Dec. 28, 1799. Lewis Tannent and Sally Clark.
Nov. 27, 1787. Jacob Umbrickhouse and Patsy Dismukes.
Nov.   2, 1786. Bowler Vawter and Sally Berry.
July 12, 1787. Richard Vawter and Sally Vaugh.
Oct. 23, 1787. Lewis Vaugh and Mary Lee.
Jan. 21, 1790. Abraham Venable and Amey Hundley.
Dec.   5, 1793. William Vaugh and Patty Vaughn.
Dec. 14, 1794. William Venable and Rebecca Hurt.
Oct. 16, 1786. James Willson and Agnes Pickett.
Jan.   7, 1789. William Wright and Fanny Riddle.
Feb.   5, 1789. William Wayt and Mary Ann Hedges.
Sept. 8, 1790. LeRoy Webster and Sarah Scanland.
Dec.   1, 1789. Elijah White and Susannah Brame.
May   22, 1790. William White and Eliza Durrett.
Jan.   2, 1790. Willis Wright and Leah Hulett.
Jan.   2, 1790. Henry Willy and Elizabeth Tinsley.
Jan.   2, 1790. Achilles Webster and Sarah Webster.
May   8, 1792. Benjamin Waller and Joana Thompson.
Oct. 21, 1792. George White and Ann Jeter.
May   19, 1793. Benjamin Whitlock and Polly Richeson.
July 19, 1794. John Willmore and Patty Tayloy.
Jan. 10, 1795. William Webster and Agnes Jones.
Feb. 11, 1795. William Willson and Delphia Foster.
Jan. 14, 1796. John Wright and Elizabeth Durrett.
Jan. 14, 1796. Nathan Winston and Ann Yarbrough.
Sept. 21, 1798. Richard Walden and Polly Isbele.
Dec. 26, 1798. James White and Elizabeth Green.
Dec. 23, 1799. Francis Wyat and Fanny Austin.
Dec. 15, 1792. James Young and Sally Jeter.
Dec. 15, 1792. John Yeatman and Lucy Patty.

EARLY SETTLERS IN VIRGINIA.

(Continued from Vol. VII.)

Daniell, Elizabeth, wife of Henry Daniel, James City, 13 November, 1635.

Darnley, William, transported by Thomas Harwood, 7 July, 1635.

David, John, transported by Capt. Thomas Willoughby, 6 November, 1635.

Davis, Thomas (servant), transported by Charles Harmar, 4 July, 1635.

Davis, William (servant), transported by John Robinson in the "Margaret & John," 1622.

Davis, William (servant), transported by William Stone of Accomac County, 4 June, 1635.

Davis, William, transported by John Upton, 7 July, 1635.

Dawkes, Henry, transported by William Swan, James City, 5 November, 1635.

Dawtres, John, transported by Jeremiah Clement, 11 June, 1635.

Day, John (servant), transported by John Slaughter, 30 May, 1635.

Davis, Richard, transported by John Arvine, 6 June, 1635.

Dawson, Thomas, transported by Capt. William Peirce, 22 June, 1635.

Deacon, Martha, transported by William Wilkinson, minister, 20 November, 1635.

Deane, Nathaniel, transported by William Barker, 26 November, 1635.

Day, Mary, transported by William Montague, Middlesex County, 7 November, 1700.

Deane, Richard, transported by John Russell, ———, 1634.

Denerell, George, transported in the "Temperance," 1621 by Lieut. Thomas Flint.

Dennie, John, transported by Thomas Harwood, 7 July, 1635.

Dennis, John, transported by Daniel Cugley, Accomac County, 25 June, 1635.

Denny, Robert, transported by George Keith, 29 July, 1635.

Depina, Lewis, transported by Sergt. Thomas Crompe of James City County, 22 September, 1635.

Dickenson, William (servant), transported by John Slaughter, 30 May, 1635.

Dickinson, Peter, transported in the "Southampton" in 1622 by John Cheesman of Elizabeth City.

Dilke, Elizabeth, wife of Capt. Clement Dilke of Accomac, transported in the "George" in 1622.

Dixon, Adam, yeoman of James City, Ann his wife and Elizabeth his daughter came in the "Margaret & John" in 1622.

Dobson, Elizabeth, transported by Miles Cary, gent., York County, 7 November, 1700.

Dodman, John (servant), transported by William Spencer, 19 June, 1635.

Dodson, Benjamin, transported by Capt. William Peirce, 22 June, 1635.

Draper, John, transported by Capt. Thomas Willoughby, 19 March, 1643.

Drawter, Ann, transported by Capt. William Peirce, 22 June, 1635.

Drew, Henry, transported by Henry Harte, 1 August, 1635.

Dunberbeach, Eleanor, transported by Thomas Harwood, 7 July, 1635.

Duning, Richard, transported by Lieut. John Cheesman, 21 November, 1635.

Dunningham, Richard, transported by Nathaniel Hooke, 5 June, 1635.

Durand, William, transported by Richard Bennett, 26 June, 1635.

Dyner, Thomas, transported by Daniel Cugley, Accomac County, 25 June, 1635.

Eaton, Nathaniel, transported by Jeremiah Clement, 11 June, 1635.

Eaton, Samuel, transported by Henry Harte, 1 August. 1635.

Eaworth, Mary, transported by Thomas Harwood. 7 July, 1635.

Edes, Alice, transported by William Swan, James City, 5 November, 1635.

Edwards, Humphrey, transported by William Woolritch, Elizabeth City, 17 June, 1635.

Edwards, William, transported by Capt. William Peirce, 22 June, 1635.

Edwards, William, transported by Capt. Adam Thorogood, 24 June, 1635.

Eggleston, transported in the "John & Dorothy" in 1634 by Capt. Adam Thorogood.

Elberry, William, transported in the "Eleanor" in 1622 by Capt. William Tucker.

Ellis, John, transported by George Menifie, 2 July, 1635.

Ellis, Samuel, transported by Robert Cane, 18 December, 1635.

Ellison, Jonathan (servant), transported by Capt. Francis Epes, 26 August, 1635.

Empson, William, transported by William Eyres, 30 June, 1635.

Enies, John, transported in the "Hopewell" in 1633, by Capt. Adam Thorogood.

Epes, Francis, son of Capt. Francis Epes, transported 26 August, 1635.

Epes, John, son of Capt. Francis Epes, transported 26 August, 1635.

Epes, Thomas, son of Capt. Francis Epes, transported 26 August, 1635.

Evans, John (servant), transported by William Gany of Accomac, 17 September, 1635.

Evans, John (servant), transported by John Sparkman, 13 July, 1635.

Evans, Morgan, transported by John Upton, 7 July, 1635.

Evans, Richard, transported from Newfoundland in the "Temperance" in 1619 by Lieut. Gilbert Peppet.

Evans, Richard, transported by William Andrews of Accomac, 25 June, 1635.

Eustis, Jeremiah, transported by Capt. William Peirce, 22 June, 1635.

Exton, William, transported by John Russell, —— 1634.

Farrar, John, transported by Capt. Thomas Willoughby, 19 November, 1635.

Farrington, Charles (servant), transported by William Stone of Accomac, 4 June, 1635.

Faune, William, transported in the "Hopewell" in 1633 by Capt. Adam Thorogood.

Fearbrace, Roger (servant), transported by William Gany of Accomac, 17 September, 1635.

Fenn, William, transported by Henry Coleman, 6 June, 1635.

Fletcher, Elizabeth, came in the "Primrose" of London in 1634, and is the wife of Hannibal Fletcher of Lower Chippoakes Creek.

Fulleroy, John, transported by Thomas Eyre of Accomac, 7 November, 1700.

Fletcher, Hannah, came in the "Middleton" in 1634, transported by Capt. Adam Thorogood.

Fletcher, James (servant), transported by William Stone of Accomac, 4 June, 1635.

Flood, John, transported by William Swan of James City, 5 November, 1635.

Flood, Richard, transported by William Swan of James City, 5 November, 1635.

Foanes, Thomas (servant), transported by Capt. Francis Epes, 26 August, 1635.

Foster, Mark, transported by William Woolritch of Elizabeth City, 17 June, 1635.

Fouke, John (servant), transported by Thomas Warren of Charles City, 20 November, 1635.

Foye, William, transported by Francis Fowler of James City County, —— 1635.

(To be continued.)

HENRICO COUNTY RECORDS.

(Continued from Vol. VII, Page 161.)

Conveyance from Philip Jones of Bristol Parish in Henrico, to William Chambers of parcel of land granted to me by my late uncle Chandler, decd. Margaret, wife of Philip Jones, renounces her dower rights. 1 February, 1688.

Indenture between Lionel Morris of New Kent, Parish of St. Peters and Daniel Price of Henrico, of one tract of land in the last named county. 26 January, 1688.

Conveyance from William Giles and Bethamah his wife, the daughter and heiress of Captain John Knowles, decd., of one parcel of land in Henrico, to John Crowley. February Court, 1688.

Deposition of Thomas Brady, aged 23 or thereabouts, that John Womeck did beat and abuse his, the said Womeck's wife without cause.

Deposition of Bartholomew Roberts, Jnr., aged 25, and Nicholas Sharp, aged 25, in re. Womeck. 1 February, 1688.

The last will and testament of Edward Stratton, Snr., dated 25 December, 1688, probated 1 February, 1688.

> To my loving wife Martha ten pounds sterling, and after all debts are paid all the rest of my goods and chattels to be divided into three parts, my wife to have one and my son two parts. My son Edward Stratton, Jnr., to be executor.

Witnesses: John Worsham, Mary Platt.

Conveyance from John Woodson, Snr., carpenter of the County and Parish of Henrico, to William Randolph of same place, of 1,800 acres of land. Judith, the wife of John Woodson, gives her consent to the sale. 30 March, 1689.

Conveyance from John Woodson, carpenter of the County and Parish of Henrico, of 200 acres of land to Benjamin Hatcher of the same place. Judith, wife of John Woodson, gives her consent to the sale. 30 March, 1689.

Inventory of the estate of Thomas Owen, decd., presented by Mr. Edward Stratton, trustee.

Deed of gift from Richard Parker of a calf to John, son of John Cannon and Esther, his wife. 1 April, 1689.

Deed of gift from Mary Gee, widow, of the County of Henrico, to her two sons Henry Gee and 'Gilbert Gee of certain household utensils. My two sons shall stay with my father until they come to 16 years and then to have their own labor and 3 breeding cattle which my father Elam will make good to them when they come to the years aforesaid. 1 April, 1689.

Will of Mathew Turpin, dated 15 January, 1688; probated April Court, 1689. My eldest son, Henry Turpin, to have all my lands, and in case of his death without heirs, then to my son designed to be named Mathew, and in case they should both decease without heirs male, my land then to revert to Mr. Thomas Osborn. Cattle and horses to be divided between my wife and children. My wife Sarah to be executrix. Witnesses: Thomas Osborn, Snr., Thomas Osborn, Jnr., John Goode, Edward Osborn.

Confirmation of a deed of land by Edward Bowman, son and heir of Robert Bowman, decd., to his brother John Bowman. 2 February, 1688.

Deposition of Thomas Farrar, aged 24 years, in the case of Mr. Stephen Cocke and Mr. Giles Webb, in that Stephen Cocke called to Thomas Farrar and Thomas Harris saying, "Bear you witness that Giles Webb calls me knave and says he will prove me one. 1 April, 1689.

Conveyance from Edward Mathews of the County of Henrico, of one parcel of land to John Pleasants. Sarah, wife of Edward Mathews, releases her dower rights. 1 April, 1689.

Administration on the estate of John Porter, decd., granted to the widow, Mary Porter, relict. 20 April, 1689.

Administration on the estate of Thomas Newcomb granted to Richard Newcomb, the brother. 20 April, 1689.

Deed of gift of a mare from Thomas Baley of the County of Henrico, planter, to Mary Jefferson, daughter of Thomas and Mary Jefferson of the County aforesaid. 1 June, 1689.

Conveyance from Thomas Cocke, Snr., to William Randolph, both of County of Henrico, of 1,650 acres of land. 1 June, 1689.

Conveyance from Thomas Cocke, Snr., and John Watson, both of Henrico, of 1,650 acres of land. 1 June, 1689.

Deed of gift from Thomas Cocke, Snr., of Henrico, to his son, James Cocke of same place, of two tracts of land. 1 June, 1689.

Conveyance from Alexander Mekenny to Humphrey Smith, of 100 acres of land. Mary, wife of said Alexander, relinquished her dower. 1 June, 1689.

Deed of gift from Samuel Knibb of Henrico, of one mare to his son, Solomon Knibb. 1 June, 1689.

Conveyance from John Coles and Susannah, his wife, of the County of Henrico, to Thomas Bayley of same place, of a parcel of land. 1 June, 1689.

Conveyance from Richard Ferris of Henrico, to James Hambleton, of a parcel of land. 1 June, 1689.

Conveyance from James Frankling of Henrico, to Peter Field of same place, of a parcel of land. 28 April, 1689.

Will of Abell Gower of the County of Henrico, gent., 25 January, 1688; probated 1 June, 1689. To my loving wife, Jane Gower, the plantation and land where I now live on for her natural life, and after her death to my daughter, Tabitha Gower, and if my daughter should die without heirs before she reach the age of 21 years, then the aforesaid land shall go to Obedience Branch and Priscilla Branch, but in default of heirs to the latter should they die before they are 21 years, then the aforesaid land to go to the next heir at law of the said Abel Gower. I also give to my daughter, Tabitha Gower, two-thirds of my goods and chattels, to be paid to her at

18 years or when she marries. My wife, Jane Gower, to be executrix. Witnesses: William Glover, Christopher Branch, Ben. Branch.

Inventory of the estate of Abell Gower, decd., taken 29 March, 1689.

Will of Edward Deely of the County of Henrico, 18 October, 1688; probated 1 June, 1689. My land and plantation to my cousin Mathew Branch, and concerning the house I am now building and all the tobacco which I have in the hands of William Glover and John Davis shall go towards the said house. To Mathew Branch my negroes. To James Branch, one cow and calf, and to each of the daughters of Thomas Branch, Jnr., one cow, and to Richard Wards daughter, one cow. To Robert Broadway, my horse, and to Dorothy Blackman, Jnr., one young mare; to William Blackman, Jnr., one black heifer; to John and Elizabeth Blackman each a cow calf. To Henrico Parish Church twenty shillings, and to John Bromfield one hogshead of tobacco; to William Blackman and Charles Douglass each one old axe. To Mr. Goode and Joshua Step the corn which they owe me; to William Glover six breeding sowes; all the other goods and chattel after my debts are paid I give to my brother, Thomas Jefferson, whom I make executor. Witnesses: Henry Sherman, William Burroughs, Henry Trent, William Glover.

Will of William Fowler, Snr., of Henrico, blacksmith, 12 March, 1688; probated 1 June, 1689. To my daughter Elizabeth Burton, one shilling. To my loving son, Samuel Fowler, all my estate it hath pleased God to endow me with, and my aforesaid son to be executor. Witnesses: William Midgley, Allanson Clerke.

Inventory of the goods of John Porter, decd., taken 18 February, 1688, presented by Mary the admx. of John Porter.

Will of Peter Harris of Henrico, 20 September, 1687; probated 1 June, 1689. To son Peter Harris one cow; to son John Harris, one cow; to daughter Michall Harris, one three year old heifer; to my daughter Anne Base, one cow called "Wolfe," and all her increase for the good of her children and to be divided amongst them when they come of age. Rest of estate to my wife Michall, and she to be the extrix. Witnesses: Thomas Cooke, Robert Woodson, Thomas East, Edward Mosby. (To be continued.)

LOUDOUN COUNTY MILITIA.
Court Order Book G.

March Court, 1778.

The following persons were recommended with rank attached. James Whaley, Jnr., 2nd Lieutenant; William Carnan, Ensign; Daniel Lewis, 2nd Lieutenant; Josias Miles, Lieutenant; Thos. King, Lieutenant; Hugh Douglas, Ensign; Isaac Vandeventer, Lieutenant; John Dodd, Ensign.

May Court, 1778.

George Summers, Colonel; Charles G. Eskridge, Colonel; Wm. McClelland, Captain; Robert McClain, Captain; John Henry, Captain; Samuel Cox, Major; Lieutenants, Francis Russell, James Beavers, Scarlet Burkley, Moses Thomas, Henry Farnsworth, John Russell, Gustavus Elgin, John Miller, Samuel Butcher, Joshua Botts, John Williams, George Tyler, Nathaniel Adams, George Mason; Ensigns, Isaac Grant, John Thatcher, William Elliott, Richard Shore, Peter Benham.

August Court, 1778.

Lieutenants, Thomas Marks, William Robison, Joseph Butler, John Linton; Ensigns, Joseph Wildman, George Asbury.

September Court, 1778.

Lieutenant, Francis Russell; Ensign, George Shrieve.

May Court, 1779.

Lieutenant, Joseph Wildman; Ensign, Francis Elgin, Jnr.

June Court, 1779.

Lieutenant, George Kilgour; Ensign, Jacob Caton.

July Court, 1779.
    Lieutenant, John Debell; Ensign, William Hutchison.
October Court, 1779.
    Captain, Francis Russell.
November Court, 1779.
    Captain, James Cleveland.   Ensign, Thomas Millan.
February Court, 1780.
    Ensign, Thomas Williams.
March Court, 1780.
    Ensign, John Benham.
June Court, 1780.
    2nd Lieutenants, Wethers Smith, William Debell;
    Ensigns, Francis Adams, Joel White.
August Court, 1780.
    Ensign, Robert Russell.
               (To be continued.)

VIRGINIA REVOLUTIONARY SOLDIERS.

Dye, Jonathan, Lieut., dec'd, Contl. Line, 3 years. Nancy
    Dye, representative, 26 November, 1783.
Morgan, Jno., Sergeant, Contl. Line, 3 years' service.
Compton, Aug., Private, Contl. Line, 3 years' service.
Murphy, Chas., Private, Contl. Line, 3 years' service.
McMechen, Robt., Private, Contl. Line, 3 years' service.
Purvis, Wm., Private, Contl. Line, 3 years' service.
Tenit, Edmund, Sergeant, Contl. Line, 3 years' service.
Parsons, Geo., Private, Contl. Line, 3 years' service.
Arnold, Jas., Private, Contl. Line, 3 years' service.
Yowell, Saml., Private, Contl. Line, 3 years' service.
Colvin, Jeremiah. Sergeant, Contl. Line, 3 years' service.
Arnold, Lewis, Private, Contl. Line, 3 years. John Arnold,
    representative, 27 November, 1783.
Sears, Thos., Private, State Line, 3 years' service.
Moore, Jno., Private, Contl. Line, 3 years' service.
Cherry, Wm., Captain, Contl. Line, 3 years' service.
George, Wm., Captain, Contl. Line, 3 years' service.
Bussell, Chas., Corporal, Contl. Line, 3 years' service.

Towns, John, Lieut., Contl. Line, 3 years' service.
Marshall, Richard, Corporal, Contl. Line, 7 years' service.
Fleet, Hy., Midshipman, State Navy, 3 years' service.
Crowder, Robt., Seaman, State Navy, 3 years' service.
Norman, Wm., Seaman, State Navy, 3 years' service.
Maughon, Geo., Seaman, State Navy, 3 years' service.
Brown, Jno., Seaman, State Navy, 3 years' service.
Ashburn, Luke, Seaman, State Navy, 3 years' service.
Foster, Wm., Private, Contl. Line, for the war.
Pitman, Geo., Sergeant, Contl. Line, 3 years' service.
McKenney, Danl., Private, Contl. Line, 3 years' service.
Wells, Jas., Private, Contl. Line, 3 years' service.
Cochran, Wm., Sergeant, Contl. Line, 3 years' service.
Smith, Thos., Private, Contl. Line, 3 years' service.
Hockaday, Philip, Lieut., Contl. Line, warrant to Jas. Hocka-
day, heir at law, 9 November, 1783.
McMahon, Roger, Private, Contl. Line, 3 years' service.
Lewis, Wm., Private, Contl. Line, 3 years' service.
Brann, Andrew, Private, Contl. Line, 3 years' service.
Griffin, Thompson, Private, Contl. Line, 3 years; warrant to
John Greffin's heir at law, December, 1783.
Humphrys, Saml., Seaman, State Navy, 3 years' service.
McIntire, Wm., Sergeant, Contl. Line, 3 years' service.
Adams, Thos., Private, Contl. Line, 3 years' service.
Watts, Gideon, Private, Contl. Line, to end of war.
Franklin, Joseph, Corporal, Contl. Line, 3 years' service.
Doil, Robt., Private, Contl. Line, 3 years' service.
Conant, Jno., Private, Contl. Line, 3 years' service.
Scott, Chas., Major-Genl., Contl. Line, 8 years' service.
Bailey, Anselm, Private, Contl. Line, 3 years' service.
Campbell, Arch., Lieut., Contl. Line, 3 years' service.
Stanley, Wm., Private, Contl. Line, 3 years' service.
Stone, Wm., Private, State Line, 3 years' service.
Tinsley, Saml., Cornet, State Line, end of war.
Grissel, Joel, Sergeant, Contl. Line, 3 years' service.
Turney, Wm., Private, Contl. Line, 3 years' service.
Angel, Baker, Sailor, State Navy, 3 years' service.
Baylie, Peter, Sailor, State Navy, 3 years' service.

Edwards, Wm., Sailor, State Navy, 3 years' service.
Russell, Wm., Col., Contl. Line, 19 Dec., 1776, to end of war.
Craig, Jas., Captain, Contl. Line, 3 years' service.
Knox, Jas., Major, Contl. Line, 3 years' service.
Thornton, Wm., Private, Contl. Line, 3 years' service.
Richardson, Richard, Private, Contl. Line, served end of the war.
Robinson, Wm., Sergeant, Contl. Line, served end of the war.
Humphrys, John, Private, Contl. Line, 3 years' service.
Moore, Nicholas, Private, Contl. Line, end of war.
Cave, Jas., Private, Contl. Line, 3 years' service.
Jeffries, Elisha, Private, Contl. Line, 3 years' service.
Beers, Jas., Private, Contl. Line, 3 years' service.
McTear, Wm., Sergeant, Contl. Line, 3 years' service.
McTear, Frizzel, Sergeant, Contl. Line, 3 years' service.
Stacey, Simon, Private, Contl. Line, 3 years' service.
Lindsey, Peter, Private, Contl. Line, 3 years' service.
Case, Wm., Private, Contl. Line, end of war.
Brahston, Wm., Private, Contl. Line, 3 years' service.
Wyne, Benj., Private, Contl. Line, 3 years' service.
Leman, Dedrick, Private, Contl. Line, 3 years' service.
Lowe, Jno., Private, Contl. Line, 3 years' service.
McDonald, Benj., Private, Contl. Line, end of war.
Denny, Hy., Sergeant, Contl. Line, 7 years' service.
Jackson, Isaac, Private, Contl. Line, 3 years' service.
Floyd, Wm., Private, Contl. Line, end of war.
McCannon, Christopher, Sergeant, Contl. Line, 3 years' service.
Fear, Jacob, Private, Contl. Line, end of war.
Feggins, Jas., Private, Contl. Line, 3 years' service.
Triplett, Nathl., Sergeant, Contl. Line, 3 years' service.
Bond, Leo, Private, Contl. Line, 3 years' service.
Kirkpatrick, A., Captain, Contl. Line, 19 February, 1776, to November 29, 1782.
Bolton, Bolling, Sergeant, Contl. Line, 3 years' service.
Brooks, Thos., Private, Contl. Line, 3 years' service.
Lucas, Saml., Private, State Line, 3 years' service.
Taylor, Chas., Private, State Line, 3 years' service.

Little, Moses, Private, State Line, 3 years' service.
Thomas, Wm., Private, State Line, 3 years' service.
Robertson, Mordicai, Private, State Line, 3 years' service.
Bozwell, Robert, Private, State Line, 3 years' service.
Bird, Thos., Private, State Line, 3 years' service.
Huey, John, Private, State Line, 3 years' service.
Lank, Jno., Private, State Line, 3 years' service.
Graham, Arthur, Private, State Line, 3 years' service.
Dixon, Jno., Drummer, State Line, 3 years' service.
Soarell, Jas., Private, State Navy, 3 years' service.
Flint, Jno., Carpenter, State Navy, 3 years' service.
House, Wm., Gunner, State Navy, 3 years' service.
Causey, Jas., Seaman, State Navy, 3 years' service.
Blundon, Wm., Sailor, State Navy, 3 years' service.
Blundon, Swann, Sailor, State Navy, 3 years' service.
Havrup, Arthur, Sergeant, Contl. Line, 3 years' service.
Hancock, Hy., Private, Contl. Line, 3 years' service.
Murfrey, Jno., Private, Contl. Line, 3 years' service.
Wilks, Burrell, Sergeant, Contl. Line, 3 years' service.
Sammon, Jno., Private, State Line, 3 years' service.
Green, Wm., Private, Contl. Line, 3 years' service.
Parish, Peter, Sergeant, Contl. Line, 3 years' service.
Payne, Jacob, Sergeant, Contl. Line, 3 years' service.
Jackson, John, Private, Contl. Line, end of war.
Jones, Godfrey, Private, Contl. Line, 3 years' service.
Hayes, Gabriel, Sergeant, Contl. Line, 3 years' service.
Gray, David, Sergeant, Contl. Line, 3 years' service.
Cookes, Michael, Private, Contl. Line, 3 years' service.
Small, Hy., Private, Contl. Line, 3 years' service.
Moore, Michael, Private, Contl. Line, 3 years' service.
Scott, Wm., Private, Contl. Line, 3 years' service.
Pile, Richard, Sergeant, Contl. Line, 3 years' service.
Craine, Jas., Captain, Contl. Line, 3 years' service.
Wright. John, Private, Contl. Line, 3 years' service.
Cassidy, Michael, Private, Contl. Line, 3 years' service.
Eakin, Saml., Sergeant, Contl. Line, 3 years' service.
Carnahan, John, Private, Contl. Line, 3 years' service.
Thompson, Patk., Sergeant, Contl. Line, 3 years' service.

Blundon, Seth, Midshipman, State Navy, 3 years' service.
Edwards, Rodham, Sailor, State Navy, 3 years' service.
Day, Geo., Sailor, State Navy, 3 years' service.
Harcum, Rodham, Midshipman, State Navy, 3 years' service.
Binns, Wm., Private, Contl. Line, 3 years' service.
Glason, Pat., Private, Contl. Line, 3 years' service.
Cruze, Redman, Private, Contl. Line, 3 years' service.
Hooper, Walter, Private, Contl. Line, end of war.
Beatley, Jas., Private, Contl. Line, 3 years' service.
Petts, Jno., Private, Contl. Line, 3 years' service.
Canary, Wm., Private, Contl. Line, 3 years' service.
Humphries, Jno., Lieut., dec'd, Contl. Line, 3 years; Sarah
    Humphries representative, 12 December, 1783.
Moshy, Wm., Private, Contl. Line, 3 years' service.
McCraw, Jno., Private, Contl. Line 3 years; Francis McCraw
    representative, 12 December, 1783.
Wood, Jno., Sergeant, Contl. Line, 3 years' service.
Honey, Elias, Private, Contl. Line, served to end of war.
Jones, Solomon, Private, Contl. Line, 3 years' service.
State, John, Captain, Contl. Line, 3 years' service.
Baily, Thos., Private, State Line, 3 years' service.
Melton, Jas., Private, State Line, 3 years' service.
Young, Saml., Private, Contl. Line, 3 years' service.
Lipscomb, Arch., Private, State Line, 3 years' service.
Johnson, John B., Captain, Contl. Line, 3 years' service.
Delozes, Aza, Private, Contl. Line, 3 years' service.

NORTHAMPTON COUNTY WILLS.

(Continued from Vol. VI.)

Smith, Richard, Northampton Co., 20 January, ———; 15
    May, 1716. Eldest son William; daus. Ann and Sarah
    Smith; sons Joshua and Richard; wife Catherine extx.
    Wit: John Luke, Andrew Andrews.
Yardly, Michall, Parish of Hungars, Northampton Co., 7
    October, 1715; 20 June, 1716. Daughters Mary and

Sarah; wife Anne extx. Wit: John Saunders, Joseph Dent, Elizabeth Jacob.

Brown, William, Northampton Co., 20 May, 1709; 20 June, 1716. Daniel Eyre, Witherington Fitchett and his sister Elizabeth; Witherington Fitchett sole extr. Wit: Sarah James, Witherington Fitchett.

Fitchett, Esther, ———;/ 14 July, 1716. Sons John, Joshua and Witherington; grandchildren Nehemiah and Comfort Fitchett; Rachel Hill; dau. Susanna Fitchett; granddaughter Elizabeth Sharp; dau. Elizabeth Sharp; son Thomas extr. Wit: William Brown, Henry Dixon, Michael Dixon.

Sanderson, John, Parish of Hungers; 20 July, 1710; 14 July, 1716. Son Thomas; wife Jane, extx. Wit: Robert Howson, William Dyer.

Frost, Thomas, Northampton Co., 30 May, 1716; 17 July, 1716. Children Thomas, Grace, Ann, Mary and Esther; wife Jane extx. Wit: Thomas Savage, George Harmanson.

Johnson, John, Northampton Co., 22 November, 1715; 17 July, 1716. Children Harman, Thomas, John, Esther and Rachel; wife Mary extx. Wit: Thomas Elliot, Snr., John Walter, Jnr., Robert Howson.

McMillan, Thomas, Northampton Co., 5 December, 1715; 17 July, 1716. John Moore; Josiah Eyre; Thomas Moore; William Satchell; Thomas Moore, Snr.; Isaac Moore; Eliz. Eyre; Thomas Eyre, Jnr., extr. Wit: Daniel Eyre, Thomas Somers, Thomas Moore, William Satchell.

Coward, Samuel. No date. 17 July, 1716. Wife Mary sold legatee. Wit: Robert Millikan, John Jackson.

Isaac, John, Northampton Co., 5 January, 1713-4; 2 August, 1716. Granddaughter Naomi Isaac; dau. Elizabeth Scott; dau. Ann Clegg; wife Naomi extx. Wit: William Hawkins, George Gorand.

Parramore, Thomas, Northampton Co., 7 July, 1713; 20 Nov. 1716. Son John; son Thomas; dau. Elizabeth; wife

Sarah extx. Wit: Robert Andrews, Mary Kitson, Mary Parramore.

Eshon, John, Northampton Co., 21 November, 1716; 18 December, 1716. Son Daniel; brother Richard Bull; cousin John Addison; wife Mary extx. Wit: Edmund Johnson, Luke Taylor, Thomas Johnson.

Capell, Nathaniel, Northampton Co., 1 August, 1713; 18 December, 1716. Son Nathaniel; dau. Esther, wife of Richard Burr; son Thomas; son Argoll; daus. Elizabeth and Hannah Capell; grandson Stratton Capell; wife Hannah extx. Wit: John Ramsbottom, Lettice Ramsbottom.

Pettit, Thomas, Northampton Co., 9 November, 1716; 18 December, 1716. Children Francis, Mary, Ann, Sarah and Elizabeth; wife Eliz. extx. Wit: Thomas Collier, Bartholomew Pettit.

Ellegood, Richard, Northampton Co., 23 October, 1715; 15 January, 1716-7. Children Edmund, Richard, Benjamin, William and Elizabeth Ellegood; wife Elizabeth extx. Wit: Benjamin Gather, Richard Waterson.

Nelson, John, Northampton Co., 7 October, 1716; 15 January, 1716-7. Daughters Anne, Elizabeth and Bethana; son John; wife Susanna extx. Wit: Joseph Tollman, William Waterson, Charles Golding.

Adison, John, Northampton Co., 29 December, 1716; 15 January, 1716-7. Sons John, Nathan, Thomas, Arnold and Isachar; daughter Bridget Nottingham; daughters Susanna and Mary; wife Barthina extx. Wit: Luke Taylor, Thomas Abdeel, Joseph Nottingham.

Taylor, Luke, planter, Northampton Co., 25 February, 1716; 19 March, 1716. Sons John and Luke; daughters Abigail and Sarah; wife (no name given) to be extx. Wit: John White, Arthur Taylor, Nath. Kellam.

Bowden, John, Northampton Co., 20 February, 1716; 16 April, 1717. Sons Peter and John; daughters Susanna and Mary; wife Susannah extx. Wit: John Stockly, James Wilton, Robert Warren, Joseph Warren.

Berry, Cornelius, Northampton Co., 24 February, 1716; 21 May, 1717. Harrison Sanderson; Esther Sanderson; sons William, Cornelius and John; wife Elizabeth extx. Wit: —— Evans, John Tatum.

Dolby, John, Northampton Co., 2 October, 1713; 17 December, 1717. Brother Joseph Dolby; cousin Ann Dolby, daughter of Joseph Dolby; brothers Benjamin and John Dolby; cousin John, son of Richard Smith; cousin Abigail, daughter of Richard Smith; cousin Thomas, son of Richard Garret; sister Sarah Garret; sister Elizabeth Johnson; wife Joanna extx. Wit: Thomas Dent, Benjamin Dolby.

Church, Thomas (Nuncupative will), 17 December, 1717. Entire estate to wife Elizabeth Church.

Wainhouse, Francis, Northampton Co., 4 December, 1717; —— January, 1717. Daughter Margaret; son Francis; my five children; wife Patience extx. Wit: Arthur Rascoe, Samuel Hardy.

Moore, Mathew, Northampton Co., 22 August, 1715; 19 February, 1717-8. Son Mathew; son Zachariah; son Thomas; daughter Elizabeth; daughter Frances; son John; daughter Leah; my son William Satchell; George Freshwater, Sr. and his son Mark; Comfort Freshwater; son Thomas Moore extr. Wit: Daniel Eyre, William Eyre, Daniel Freshwater.

Savage, Benjamin, Northampton Co., 23 October, 1717; 18 February, 1717-8. Sons John and Littleton; daughter Sarah; child my wife now goes with; wife Susannah to be extx. Wit: Bridget Savage, Luke Johnson.

Banks, Harrison, Northampton Co., 15 January, 1717; 18 April, 1717-8. Wife Joan entire estate. Wit: Thomas Banks, Thomas Savage.

Freshwater, George, Northampton Co., 26 October, 1717; 17 March, 1717-8. Sons George, Thomas, Mark and Mathew; daughters Rose and Sarah; daughter Elizabeth Rasco; granddaughter Comfort Freshwater; wife Eliz.

extx. Wit: John Eyre, Daniel Eyre, William Eyre, Samuel Burton.

Dowman, Daniel, Northampton Co., 15 December, 1717; May Court, 1718. Brother Nathl. Dowman; my mother now living; Eliz. Dowman; brothers Jacob and John Dowman; sister Esther Dowman; sister Margaret Dowman; brother Nathaniel extr. Wit: Arthur Rasco, Richard Smith, John Moore.

Powell, John, Northampton Co., 1 June, 1718; June Court, 1718. Daughters Sarah, Rose, Yardley, Mary and Margaret Powell; wife Sarah extx. Wit: Robert Sill, Esther Mapp, George Harmanson, John Douglas.

White, John, Northampton Co., 26 May, 1718; June Court, 1718. Daughters Temperance and Elizabeth; son Obedience; wife Ann extx. Wit: John Marshall, William Stokes, John Tilney.

Banks, Thomas, Northampton Co., 12 March, 1717; June Court, 1718. Sons Robert and William; daughters Grace and Ann; wife Sarah extx. Wit: Richard Thorman, Joseph Warren, Littleton Robins.

Golding, William, Jr., Northampton Co., 16 April, 1718; July Court, 1718. To Thomas Fox; to my father; wife Elizabeth extx. Wit: George Knight. Richard Bull, John White.

Andrews, Robert, Northampton Co., 23 June, 1718; 17 Sept.. 1718. Sons John, Jacob, Nathaniel, Robert and Southey Roberts; daughters Sarah and Rachel; sons Robert and Nathl. extrs. Wit: James Fairfax, Rich. Booth, Thos. Gascoigne, Thos. James.

Jacob, Risdon, Northampton Co., 14 August, 1718; 17 September, 1718. My seven children Lazarus, Isaac, Thomas, Rachel, Abraham, Leah and Jacob; wife Bridget extx. Wit: John Robins, William Waterson, John Waterson, Robert Foster.

Leady, Anthony, Northampton Co., 13 August, 1718; 17 September, 1718. Sons Stephen and John; son-in-law Joseph Dunton; daughters Charity and Patience; daughter-in-law Comfort Dunton; daughter Elizabeth; wife Eliz. extx. Wit: Luke Johnson, John Johnson.

Teague, Simon, Northampton Co., 26 August, 1718; 17 September, 1718. Cousin Simon Johnson; cousin Obedience Johnson; cousin Barth. Coizer; neighbor Alice Green and her son Joseph; cousin Eliz. Reed; cousin Benj. Johnson; cousin Eliz. Gill; cousins Peter, Roland and Jasper Douty; cousin Obedience Johnson extr. Wit: Arthur Rasco, Thomas Fisher, Sarah Fisher.

Eliott, Thomas, Snr., Northampton Co., 22 July, 1718; 22 October, 1718. Son Thomas; daughter Abigail, wife Mary extx. Wit: Elizabeth Griffith, D. Newton.

Powell, Sarah, Northampton Co., 11 October, 1718; 19 November, 1718. Daughters Rose, Margaret and Isabel Powell; daughter Sarah extx. Wit: Walter Dickson, Esther Mapp, George Harmanson.

LYON FAMILY.
RECORDS FROM HENRY, HALIFAX AND PITTSYLVANIA COUNTIES.

At the first Court held for Henry county, 20 April, 1778, James Lyon is appointed Major in the room of Abraham Penn.

At a Court held for Henry county March, 1779, Eliphaz Shelton is appointed Captain in the room of James Lyon; Stephen Lyon is appointed first Lieutenant, William Holbert second Lieutenant and David Rogers, Ensign.

At a Court held for Henry county March, 1779, James Lyon is paid 100 lbs. of tobacco for one wolf head.

At a Court held for Henry county August, 1779, Patrick Henry, Hugh Innes, Archelaus Hughes, Robert Hairston, Edmund Lyne, Abraham Penn, John Slamon, James Lyon, Robert Woods, Jesse Heard, Jonathan Hanby, Peter Saunders, William Tunstall, George Waller, Frederick Reeves, William Cook, Thomas Henderson, John Fontaine, Henry Lyne, John Dillard, John Marr and William Letcher are recommended to His Excellency the Governor as proper persons to serve on the Commission of the Peace for this county.

At a Court held for Henry county May, 1782, James Lyon is granted 20/- for 100 lbs. of beef for Captain Eliphaz Shelton's company on their march against the Tories.

At a Court held for Henry county March, 1780, William Tunstall, Esq., having resigned his office as county Lieutenant; Archelaus Hughes, Esq., Colonel is advanced to the said office, and Abraham Penn, Esq., Lieutenant-Colonel to the office of Colonel; and James Lyon, Esq., to the office of Lieutenant-Colonel.

At a Court held for Henry county June, 1780, George Waller, Esq., is appointed Major in the room of James Lyon, Esq.

At a Court held for Henry county 29 March, 1783, James Lyon, Esq., produced a commission from the Governor appointing him Lieutenant-Colonel of the Militia of this county, and took the usual oaths.

Deed dated 22 July, 1784, from James Lyon to John Fletcher, 36 acres of land on Matthews Creek in said county of Henry.

Deed dated 22 July, 1784, from James Lyon of Henry county to James Mankin, 216 acres of land on north side of Russell creek in said county.

Deed dated 27 September, 1786, from Palatiah Shelton of Henry county to Stephen Lyon, 50 acres of land on the north side of Russell creek, adjoining that of James Lyon.

Deed dated 13 October, 1788, from James Lyon to Stephen Lyon, 3 tracts of 200 acres, 54 acres and 316 acres on Russell creek.

Deed dated 10 September, 1788, from Palatiah Shelton of Henry county to Stephen Lyon, 1 tract of 204 acres, 1 tract of 251 acres and 1 tract of 109 acres on Russell creek.

Deed dated 28 December, 1789, from James Lyon of Henry county to Miller Woodson Easley, that "for and in consideration of the good will, natural affection, etc., that I bear to my daughter Mary Easley, wife of the said Miller Woodson Easley," a tract of land on both sides of Mayo river, containing 167 acres.

Deed dated 12 April, 1790, from James Lyon of Henry county to Humbertson Lyon his son, "that for the good will he bears for his son Humbertson Lyon," 222 acres of land on Russell creek.

Deed dated 30 August, 1790, from Stephen Lyon of Henry county to Robert Wilson, conveying in trust, 190 acres and 360 acres on Snow creek in North Carolina, also certain negroes to secure the payment of 600 pounds.

Deed dated —— 1790, from Stephen Lyon of Henry county to James Campbell and Luke Wheeler, merchants of Petersburg, Va., 1200 acres "which he purchased of his father and Palatiah Shelton."

Deed dated —— 1790, from James Lyon of the county of Patrick, Va., makes power of attorney for the collection from John Henderson and Barna Wells, what they owe him as his Deputy-Sheriffs for the years 1786 and 1787.

Deed dated 21 February, from William R. Hinton of Pittsylvania county to James Lyon of same place, 54 acres of land lying on Russells creek.

Deed dated 2 July, 1773, from Francis Childs of Pittsylvania county to James Lyon of same place, 200 acres of land lying on the waters of Mayo river.

Deed dated 14 August, 1765, from Charles Perkins of Rowan county, North Carolina to James Lyon of Halifax county, Va., one parcel of land situated on both sides of Russells creek in the above county of Halifax, containing about 200 acres of land. Recorded at a Court held for Halifax county, 17 July, 1766.

VOL. IX. (Old Series)
VOL. I. (New Series)   YEAR 1911   Parts 2—3

Virginia
County Records

AND

Heraldic Quarterly Register

OF

THE UNITED STATES AND CANADA

Official Publication of the College of Arms of Canada

EDITED BY

William Armstrong Crozier, F. R. S., F. G. S. A.

The Genealogical Association, Publishers
Hasbrouck Heights
New Jersey

NOTICE TO SUBSCRIBERS.

The Virginia County Records Quarterly Magazine has been designated as the Official Publication of the College of Arms of Canada, and henceforth will be known as the "Virginia County Records and Heraldic Quarterly Register" of the United States and Canada. The volume for 1911 being the first volume of the new series.

The policy of the publishers to print the old records of the Colony of Virginia will be adhered to, but the value of the publication will be enhanced by the additional Heraldic data, which will cover the armigerous families of the United States and Canada.

Certificates and confirmations of arms under Seal of the College are granted to all those who can prove descent from an armigerous ancestor, upon payment of the fees for certification.

There are no fees to be paid, unless the applicant is granted a certificate.

Residents of the United States may make application through the Deputy-Commissioner, William Armstrong Crozier, F.R.S., F.G.S.A., Hasbrouck Heights, New Jersey.

College of Arms of Canada

Founded by Edict of King Louis XIV., in 1664. Confirmed by
Royal Commission of the Appeal of Malta 1877.

OFFICERS.

The Baron de Longueuil, Chancellor of the Aryan and Seigneuria.
Orders.

The Viscount de Fronsac, Herald-Marshal, Huntingdon, P. Q., Canada,
Hon. Thomas Scott Forsyth, Registrar-General, 19 Hanover Street.
Montreal, Canada.

COMMISSIONERS.

Henry Black Stuart, Esq., C. E., Sexton Villa, Westmount,
Montreal, Canada.
Rev. J. B. Pyke, M. A., 19 Hanover Street. Montreal, Canada.

SOLICITOR-GENERAL IN THE UNITED STATES.

Sir John Calder Gordon, 17 Milk Street, Boston, Mass.

DEPUTY COMMISSIONER IN THE UNITED STATES.

William Armstrong Crozier, Esq., F. R. S., F. G. S. A.,
Hasbrouck Heights, N. J.

YELLOW ROSE PERSUYVANT.

J. G. B. Bulloch, Esq., M. D., 2122 P. Street, N. W.
Washington, D. C.

REPRESENTATIVE IN GREAT BRITAIN.

The Marquis de Ruvigny, 14 Hanover Chambers, Buckingham St.,
Strand, W. C., London.

REPRESENTATIVE IN FRANCE.

M. Louis Denys de Bonaventure, Chateau d'Aytre, Charente Inferieure.

OFFICIAL PUBLICATION.

The Virginia County Records and Heraldic Quarterly Register of the
United States and Canada.

CONTENTS.

Virginia County Records

HERALDIC AND QUARTERLY REGISTER

| VOL. IX (OL.D SERIES)
VOL. I (NEW SERIES) | 1911 | Parts 2 and 3 |

INDEX TO LAND GRANTS

GLOUCESTER COUNTY.

(Continued from Vol. VII.)

BOOK No. 6.

159	Thos. Miller 1665	390
172	Richard Dudley 1665	944
187	Peter Richardson and the heirs of James .	
	Roe 1672	1500
191	John Shapley 1668	350
211	Thos. Purnell and John Benson........1668	950
231	Geo. Pead 1671	150
235	Chas. Roane 1669	150
235	Chas. Roane 1668	761
240	Lawrence Smith 1668	75
240	Thos. Buckner and Thos. Royston......1669	1000
241	John Curtis 1668	160
242	Robert Beverley 1669	116
243	Richard Lee 1668	450
250	Diana Moone, relict of John Oxford,	
	dec'd. 1669	100
250	Sara Long and Mary Shipley, daughters	
	of Abraham English, dec'd. 1669	350
253	Nathan Fletcher 1670	240
264	Cornelius Reynolds 1669	180
277	Wm. Peach 1669	570
279	Nath. Fletcher 1669	320
884	Thos. Vicars and Robert Littlefield....1669	550
284	Thos. Collins 1669	250
327	Nicholas Wrenn 1664	100
381	Thos. Deacon 1671	
	Land given by Thos. Bremo to Margaret	
	Bremo, his wife and found to escheat.	
383	Hugh Newett 1671	1170
411	Wm. Howard 1672	108
414	Philip Hunley 1672	460
426	Thos. Stephens 1672	175
428	Wm. Elliott, Sr. 1672	1100
429	Lambert Moore and Bartholomew Ram-	
	sey 1672	350
429	Mathew Gayle 1672	284
438	Geo. Harper 1672	133

438	Robert Beverley	1672	500
438	Mary Kibble, daughter of Geo. Kibble, dec'd.	1672	500
439	Richard Bailey	1672	882
442	Richard Dudley	1672	944
448	Wm. Herst	1672	363
448	Edmund Pare	1672	77
449	Jóhn Gylon	1672	188
453	Thos. Ryland	1673	120
470	Chas. Roan	1673	100
470	John Goodson	1673	100
472	Thos. Hancks	1673	264
475	Richard Shapley, son of John and Mary Shapley	1673	130
475	Wm., son of Lt.-Col. Anthony Elliot, dec'd.	1673	340
476	Thos. Hancks	1673	500
476	John Shapley	1673	430
476	Guy Knight	1673	423
479	Peter Arundell	1673	350
479	Major Robert Bristow	1673	930
490	Robert Beverley	1673	1500
494	Robert Beverley	1673	920
494	Thos. Putnam	1673	333
494	Robert Beverley	1673	150
511	Henry Wright, son and heir of John Wright, dec'd.	1674	140
511	Thos. Hankes and Cornelius Cheesman	1674	260
511	Saml Clerk	1674	700
512	Richard Dudley	1674	980
514	George Billipps	1674	500
514	Wm. Snapes	1674	110
515	Alexander, son of Wm. Snelling, dec'd.	1674	43
523	Major Richard Lee	1674	1140
524	John Leeke	1674	83
536	Edward Pore	1674	150
536	Capt. John Armistead	1674	440

537	Jas. Stubbins	1674	450
547	Richard Bailey	1674	1875
548	Thos. Graves and Jeffrey Graves, sons of Thos. Graves, dec'd.	1674	440
548	Dunken Bohannon	1674	340
549	Stephen Fentry	1674	300
549	Danl Langham	1674	350
549	John Guyton	1674	313
549	Jas. Lindsay	1674	390
549	John Nevill (infant)	1674	100
550	Mathew Kemp, Jr.	1674	229
551	John Green	1674	600
551	Jacob Johnson	1674	740
551	Col. Mathew Kemp	1674	573
552	Geo. Curtis	1674	800
554	Robert Bennett	1674	330
557	Philip Lightfoot	1675	150
557	Lewis Day	1675	400
558	Capt. Robert Beverley	1675	698
559	Francis Broughton	1675	170
559	Leonard Ambrose	1675	60
559	David, son of Major David Cant, dec'd.	1675	1400
560	Walter, son of Major David Cant, dec'd.	1675	500
560	Thos. Sewell	1675	150
591	Mary Dickeson	1676	930
592	Wm. Tomson	1676	150
601	Wm. Anderson	1676	60
601	Jas. Reynolds	1676	140
601	Susanna Wells (infant)	1676	57

Adjoining the land of John Wells, dec'd which said land was formerly surveyed for the use of Edward Wells, dec'd, father of John Wells.

622	Edmund Gwinn	1672	80
623	Mary Tittertun	1678	930
646	Wm. Crimes	1678	450
649	Thos. Vicaris	1678	190

649	Edmund, William and John Dobson, sons of Edward Dobson, dec'd. 1678	1150
657	Lt.-Col. John Armistead 1678	220
658	John Degge 1678	1800
658	Archibald Bromley 1678	500
658	John Tillett and Giles Vandecasteel....1678	25
659	Wm. Beard 1678	380
659	Christopher Dickens 1678	160
659	John Degge 1678	200
659	John Collis 1678	620
660	Ralph Armistead 1678	48
660	John Waters 1678	140
660	Lawrence Peirott 1678	137
660	Philip Hunley, Jr. 1678	200
661	Richard Longest 1678	680
661	Robert Lendall 1678	150
665	Col. Thos. Pate 1678	200
666	Thos. Amis 1678	295
666	Capt. John Armistead 1678	550
666	Wm. Noman 1678	1777½
666	Robert Beverley 1678	300
674	Capt. John Armistead 1679	550
679	Daniel Gohon 1679	100
679	John Pickering 1679	197
679	Thos. Ryland 1679	240
679	George Axe 1679	157½
681	Francis Jarvis 1679	150
682	John Waters 1679	500

BOOK VII.

1	George Burgh 1679	170
1	Richard Creedle 1679	220
2	John Armistead 1679	500
3	Mrs. Eliz. Bannister for life and then to son John Bannister, son and heir of John Bannister, dec'd. 1679	1600
4	Edward Munford 1679	80

8	Wm. Humphrey and John Tomkins, sons of Humphrey Tomkins, dec'd	1679	217½
15	Peter White, the land formerly taken up by Lambert Moore and Bartho. Ramsey	1679	350
36	Wm. Snapes	1680	75
64	Major Lewis Burwell	1680	3400
82	Wm. Skelton	1681	150
83	Chas. Roan	1681	700
115	John Buckner	1681	300
161	Archibald Bromley	1682	400
162	Thos. Boswell	1682	1100
163	Abraham Bradley	1682	150
212	John Buckner and Major Henry Whiteing	1682	2673
212	Edward Baram (orphan)	1682	364
213	John Lyllie	1682	234
214	Wm. Hoggin	1682	15
214	Richard Billops	1682	92
214	Wm. Morgan	1682	50
215	John Peade, orphan of George Peade	1682	317
218	John Bartlett	1682	50
219	Robert Cully and Ralph Armistead	1682	63½
220	Walter Morgan	1682	201
220	Morris Mackashannock	1682	140
222	Edward Lassell	1682	335
223	Sands Knowles	1682	230
230	Edward Mumford	1682	25
233	Robert Peyton	1682	150
245	Henry, son and heir of John Fox, dec'd	1683	300
275	Geo. Billops	1683	750
278	John Smither	1683	890
279	John Deggs	1683	1425
286	Abraham Bradley	1683	61
287	George Billops	1683	186
288	Peter Starling	1683	300
289	John Garnett	1683	260

643 Mary, Eliz. and Ann Howard, daus. of
       Thos. Howard, dec'd. 1688   180
685 Motrom Wright 1688   1000
688 John Dickenson, formerly granted to
       Mary Dickenson, alias Titterton, dec'd. 1688   188
685 Motrom Wright 1688   1000
688 John Dickenson, formerly granted to
       Mary Dickenson, alias Titterton, dec'd. 1688   930
684 Chas. Roane 1688   797
707 Ralph Wormeley ....——   83

Book No. 8.

 16 Robert Prior 1689   309
 17 Christopher Greenaway 1689   445
 17 Augustine Horth 1689   441
 98 Richard Barnard 1690   1090
 99 Lawrence Perrot 1690   340
140 John Armistead 1691   80
142 Saml. Norrington in right of his wife
       Hannah 1691   540
144 Wm. Fleming 1691   600
148 Wm. Collaine, Jr. 1691   140
158 John Guthry 1691   200
159 Henry Wareing 1691   152
192 Charles Roane 1691   164
192 Charles Roane 1691   278
193 Wm. Brookin and Rob't Netles........1691   270
193 Wm. Brookin 1691   517
194 Wm. Heyward 1691   156
194 John Baker 1691   40
195 Thos. Vicaris, clerk 1691   150
195 Wm. Hall 1691   220
204 John Buckner, Sr. 1691   3125
206 Richard Glasscock 1691   335
212 Major Lawrence Smith 1691   1200
215 Robert Lee 1662   542
234 Robert, son of Major Robert Beverley,
       dec'd. 1692   200

425	Geo. Williams	1701	100
438	Peter Beverley	1702	230
439	Robt. Bryan, a minor, son of Robt. Bryan, dec'd.	1702	57
457	John Stubbs	1702	100
490	Robert Carter	1702	130
535	John Stubbs	1703	50
542	Mordecai Cook	1703	1200
565	Saml. Vaudery	1703	400
588	Anne Forrest	1704	200
589	Wm. Thornton, Jr.	1704	110
591	Dunken Bohannon	1704	145
591	Wm. Callawne	1704	62
595	John Lander	1704	250
601	Col. Jas. Ransone	1704	40
603	Robert Porteous	1704	692
614	Robt. Bryan, son of Robt. Bryan, dec'd.	1704	60
615	Michel Parratt	1704	110
621	Ambrose Dudley	1704	212
695	Geo. Janson	1705	100
700	Henry Armistead	1705	202½
729	Geo. Billops	1706	335

BOOK 10.

6	John Smith, Esq.	1711	51
13	John Lewis, John Smith of Purton, and John Washington, Jr., of Westmoreland	1711	46½
15	John Spinks	1711	464
49	Wm. Smith	1711	150
56	Anne and Mary Sterling	1711	400
122	Thos. Cooke	1713	300
123	Thos. Cooke	1713	156
127	Richard Parrett	1714	43
173	Thos. Reade	1714	47
214	John Stubbs	1714	300
219	Christopher Dickens	1714	20

Book 41.
253 Nicholas Lewis 1773   23
Book 42.
536 Robert Spratt 1774   50
Book B.
404 Nicholas Lewis 1780   44
Book H.
30   Peter Beverley Whiting, heir at law of
       Peter B. Whiting, dec'd..............1783   388
315 Philip Tabb 1783   276
Book I.
505 Isaac Armistead 1784   400
Book 22.
295 Matthew Anderson 1790   8½
Book 42.
224 John Southgate 1799   110

———

DINWIDDIE COUNTY.
(Continued from Vol. VI.)
496 Thos. Goodwin 1758   71
496 Thos. Goodwin 1758   80
497 Roger Daniel, Jr....................1758   33¼
497 Geo. Smith 1758   19½
499 Isaac Tucker 1758   47½
501 Wm. Perkins 1758   45
501 Chas. Turnbull 1758   27
508 John Browder, Jr...................1758   10
522 John Browder, Jr...................1758   299
557 Wm. Raney 1759   250
591 Thos. Gent 1759   20
625 Jas. Burdge 1759   400
626 Joseph Butler 1759   120
666 John Pemberton 1760   108
804 Joshua Pritchard, Jr.................1760   177
834 Peter Williams 1760   46½

861	John Jones	1760	312
880	John Spain	1760	200
880	John Goodwin	1760	381
881	John Goodwin	1760	114
889	Avis Overby	1760	121
889	Robert Tucker	1760	132
895	Chas. Roper	1760	39½
1033	Alex Bolling	1761	897
1039	Jas. Roper	1761	44
1075	Ralph Jackson, Jr.	1761	177
439	Anne Fitzgerald	1758	182

BOOK 34.

151	Wm. Scoggin	1756	242
155	Wm. Cryer	1756	200
186	Jas. Roisseau	1757	628
208	Roger Atkinson	1757	99
208	Zacharias Fenn	1757	38
209	Morris Vaughan	1757	65
209	Joseph Westmoreland	1757	27
242	John Butler	1759	120
306	Arthur Watts	1759	126
310	Wm. Wells	1759	318
330	John Hardaway	1759	195
351	John Crew	1759	150
356	Robert Warren	1759	239
357	Wm. Pettypool	1759	400
357	Wm. Pettypool	1759	165
397	Harwood Goodwin	1759	300
399	Thos. Smith	1759	239
419	Jacob Trabue	1759	393
434	Harwood Goodwin	1759	213
435	Harwood Goodwin	1759	400
447	Richard Overby, Jr.	1759	316
488	Thos. Jones	1760	104
503	Theodorick Bland	1760	2089
555	Roger Atkinson	1760	1190

567	Wm. Eaton	1760	110½
623	Joshua Wynne	1760	122
755	John Carter	1760	114
775	Peter Thomas, Jr.	1760	230
776	Robert West	1760	100
793	Joseph Gibson	1761	400
795	Thos. Williams	1761	300
796	Joseph Gibson	1761	204
841	Alex. Bolling	1761	1500
934	David Aberneathy	1761	67
1018	Thos. Short	1762	250

Book 35.

21	Robert Hutchings	1762	16
64	Daniel Spain	1762	239
85	Thos. Williams	1763	1315½
87	Thos. Williams	1763	400
296	Leonard Claiborne, Jr.	1763	225
304	John Hardy	1763	96
451	John Beal	1763	9½

Book 36.

647	Wm. Price	1764	76
741	Peter Warren	1765	189
762	Wm. Harper	1765	400
853	Roger Atkinson	1765	137
875	Robert Ruffin	1765	107
919	Tamer Overby	1765	4¼

Book 37.

23	John Peterson	1767	24
451	Wm. Woodward	1768	400

Book 38.

466	Jas. Hardaway	1768	369
621	David Williams	1769	68½
694	Geo. Archer	1769	212
849	Wm. Watkins	1769	23¾

Book 39.

211	Thos. Barrett	1770	28

BOOK 40.

660	Jas. Butler	1772	34½
665	Jno. Hardaway	1772	51

BOOK 41.

11	Jesse Lee	1772	14
25	Edmond and Anne Perkins	1772	25
109	Moses Ingram	1773	774
165	Drury Burdge	1773	269
277	Matt. Marrable	1773	90
319	Richard Cross	1773	92
332	Isham Eppes	1773	2
333	Francis Eppes	1773	7
409	Alex Shaw	1773	25

BOOK 42.

457	John Jones	1773	23½
477	John Trabue	1773	45
675	Alex Shaw	1774	4
729	John Roberts	1774	51
747	Francis Eppes	1774	400
797	Thos. Westmoreland	1774	18
812	Gray Briggs	1774	878
814	Joseph Buffinton Darwell	1774	32

BOOK A.

328	Peter Poythress	1780	13

BOOK B.

144	Jas. Greenway	1779	129
146	Jas. Greenway	1779	357
173	Jas. Greenway	1779	99¾
448	Wm. Call	1780	356

BOOK C.

312	Joseph Jones	1781	1 lot
313	John Grammar	1781	1 acre

BOOK D.

514	Thos. Anderson	1781	10

Book E.
545 Martha Bough 1780   85

Book F.
71   Peter Randolph 1780   1

Book H.
61   Wm. Thompson 1783   100
371 Thos. Overby 1783   11
535 Jas. Overby 1783   10

Book M.
308 Wm. Honnicutt 1784   35

Book N.
52   Col. Joseph Jones 1784   170
194 Wm. Malone 1784   83

Book S.
514 Wm. Cole 1785   293

Book V.
198 Beverly Brown 1785 1434½

Book Y.
470 Jas. Greenway 1786   200

Book 11.
690 Jas. Greenway 1787   250

Book 14.
242 Kennon Jones 1787   1 lot

Book 16.
693 Jas. Greenway 1788   69

Book 20.
313 Jesse Lee 1789   520

Book 22.
90   Adam Wells 1790   68

Book 25.
185 Thos. Hardaway 1791   134
186 John Perkins 1791   25

Book 27.
682 Thos. Kirby 1793   85½
     Lamb, Wm. Lamb, Danl. Lamb, Robt.

Book 28.
531 Wm. Perkins 1793   49

Book 29.
501 Richard Troublefield 1794   16
502 Jas. Greenway 1794   46½

Book 32.
79 Jesse Bonner 1794   12

Book 33.
424 Jno. Eppes Lamb, Patsy Eppes Lamb, Eliz.
     Lamb and Thos. Hamlington Lamb, heirs
     to Thos. Lamb, dec'd 1796   29

Book 34.
221 Duncan Rose, exr. of John Banester, dec'd.1796   18

Book 36.
35 Robert Bolling 1796   1½

Book 38.
30. John Baird, Jr.....................1797   16
91 Winkfield Mason 1798   19
523 Peter Vaughan 1798   112
606 Humphrey Taylor 1799   3½

Book 39.
20 John Perkins 1797   41

Book 40.
506 Geo. Pegram 1798   253

Book 41.
37 John Mingee 1798   41
235 John Hitchcock 1799   4½
233 James Lunciford 1799   1½

Book 42.
364 Robert Atkinson 1799   10

LOUDOUN COUNTY MILITIA.

(Continued from page 23.)

October Court, 1780.

John Spitzfathem, 1st Lieutenant; Thomas Thomas and Mathew Rust, 2nd Lieutenant; Nicholas Minor, Jnr., David Hopkins, William McGeath and Samuel Oliphant, Ensigns; Charles Bennett, Captain.

November Court, 1780.

James Coleman, Esq., Colonel; George West, Lieutenant Colonel; James McIlhaney, Major.

February Court, 1781.

Simon Triplett, Colonel; John Alexander, Lieutenant Colonel; Jacob Reed, Major; John Linton, Captain; William Debell and Joel White, Lieutenants; Thomas Minor, Ensign; Thomas Shores, Captain; John Taylor and Thomas Beaty, Lieutenants; John McClain, Ensign.

March Court, 1781.

John McGeath, Captain; Ignatius Burnes, Captain; Hugh Douglas, 1st Lieutenant; John Cornelison, 2nd Lieutenant; Joseph Butler and Conn O'Neale, Lieutenants; John Jones, Jnr., Ensign; William Taylor, Major of the 1st Battalion; James Coleman, Colonel; George West, Lieutenant Colonel; Josiah Maffett, Captain; John Binns, 1st Lieutenant; Charles Binns, Jnr., 2nd Lieutenant; Joseph Hough, Ensign.

April Court, 1781.

Samson Trammell, Captain; Spence Wiggington and Smith King, Lieutenants.

May Court, 1781.

Thomas Respess, Esq., Major; Hugh Douglas, Gent., Captain; Thomas King, Lieutenant; William T. Mason, Ensign; Samuel Noland, Captain; Abraham Dehaven and Enoch Thomas, Lieutenants; Isaac Dehaven and Thomas Vince, Ensigns; James McIlhaney, Captain; Thomas Kennan, Captain; John Bagley, 1st Lieutenant.

June Court, 1781.
Enoch Furr and George Rust, Lieutenant; Withers Berry and William Hutchison, Ensigns.

September Court, 1781.
Gustavus Elgin, Captain; John Littleton, Ensign.

January Court, 1782.
William McClellan, Captain.

February Court, 1782.
William George, Timothy Hixon and Joseph Butler, Captains.

March Court, 1782.
James McIlhaney, Captain; George West, Colonel; Thomas Respess, Lieutenant Colonel.

July Court, 1782.
Samuel Noland, Major; James Lewin Gibbs, 2nd Lieutenant; Giles Turley, Ensign.

August Court, 1782.
Enoch Thomas, Captain; Samuel Smith, Lieutenant; Matthias Smitley, 1st. Lieutenant; Charles Tyler and David Beaty, Ensigns.

December Court, 1782.
Thomas King, Captain; William Mason, 1st Lieutenant; Silas Gilbert, Ensign.

———————

ORANGE COUNTY MARRIAGE BONDS.
(Continued from Vol. VII, page 167.)

Feb. 11, 1784. Madison Breedlove and Judy Buckner.

July 21, 1758. William Bledsoe and Sally, dau. of Elijah Morton. Security Aaron Bledsoe.

Sept. 14, 1785. Thomas Bibb and Sarah, dau. of Samuel Brockman.

Jan. 13, 1786. Robert Alcock and Mary Bell, widow.

Mar. 1, 1786. Silence Atkins and Frances, dau. of John Jennings.

Jan. 13, 1786. Larkin Ballard and Elizabeth, dau. of Sally Gaines.

Oct. 30, 1786. Alexander Balmain and Lucy, dau. of Erasmus Taylor.

May, 30, 1786. William Beall, Jnr., and Hannah Gordon. Security John Gordon.

Feb. 23, 1786. William Bell and Elizabeth Johnson.

Aug. 24, 1786. Patrick Bray and Mary, dau. of Thomas Stocks.

Oct. 17, 1786. Thomas Broughton and Sarah Kamp.

Nov. 1, 1786. Archibald Campbell and Susannah Arnold.

Dec. 18, 1786. James Coleman and Molly Chew.

Jan. 7, 1786. Francis Coleman and Betsy, dau. of Joseph and Elizabeth Davis.

Feb. 28, 1786. Beverly Daniel and Jane Hiatt.

Mar. 11, 1786. Jonathan Joseph and Sarah, dau. of Robert Deering.

Nov. 20, 1786. Spencer Menifee and Betta Boston. Security Joseph Boston.

Mar. 23, 1786. Moses Perry and Susan Brockman. Security Samuel Brockman.

Jan. 24, 1786. John Poulter and Patsy Ransdell. Security Sanford Ransdell.

Dec. 15, 1786. Joel Rucker and Nancy ————

Aug. 26, 1786. Edward Smith and Rose Warren.

Mar. 20, 1786. Beverly Stanton and Jemima, dau. of Betty Stanton.

Nov. 24, 1786. Samuel Steele and Mary McQuiddy.

Nov. 10, 1786. Henry Stone and Nancy, dau. of William Golding.

Nov. 2, 1786. John Stockdell, Jnr. and Sally Duvall.

Dec. 11, 1786. Jesse Tinder and Aliapear Abell.

Oct. 11, 1786. Abner Watson and Elizabeth, dau. of Catherine Dear.

Nov. 15, 1786. Jonathan White and Elizabeth Townsend.

Mar. 25, 1786. Jacob Williams and Mary Delaney.

April 23, 1787. James Allen and Patsy Woolfork.

Jan. 9, 1787. Joseph Atkins and Ann Atkins.

Nov. 24, 1787. William Cooper and Mary, dau. of Moses Quisenberry.

July 3, 1787. John Bell and Judith Burnley.

Mar. 22, 1787. Thomas Barbor and Mary Taylor. Security James Taylor.

Aug. 13, 1787. Francis Cowherd and Lucy, dau. of John Scott.

Feb. 10, 1787. Robert Dickinson and Ruth, dau. of Joseph Parish.

Nov. 14, 1787. Stephen Fitzgerald and Catherine, dau. of Samuel Bruce.

Nov. 26, 1787. John Head and Nancy, dau. of Ann Sanford.

May 5, 1787. William Herndon and Sukey Perry.

Nov. 15, 1787. Zachariah Jones and Rebecca Deane.

Dec. 20, 1787. Jacob Lauton and Hannah Webb.

July 23, 1787. John Michie and Frances, dau. of Theodosia Early. Security James Early.

Nov. 3, 1788. Jonathan Pitcher and Betsey Mason.

Nov. 27, 1788. James Riddell and Theodosia Rhodes.

May 6, 1789. Elliott Rucker and Nancy Smith.

Nov. 3, 1788. Rice Pendleton and Elizabeth Quisenberry. Security George Quisenberry.

Sept. 10, 1789. John Pearson and Betsy Goddridge.

Sept. 1, 1788. Willis Overton and Nancy Bradley.

Dec. 3, 1789. James Page, with consent of Elizabeth Page and Winny, dau. of Elizabeth Shifflet.

Oct. 2, 1788. Beverley Overton and Elizabeth Conner. Security Willis Overton.

Sept. 15, 1789. Beverley Overton and Patsy, dau. of William Richards. (Note.—This is evidently a 2nd marriage, as application of B. Overton is same handwriting as the first.)

April 24, 1788. John Morton and Mary Tandy. Security Henry Tandy.

June 9, 1789. Reuben Mallory and Dorothy (Cartel?).

Mar. 10, 1788. George McCoy and Elizabeth, dau. of Nathan Nickings.

Dec. 8, 1789. John Mothers and Sukey Burras.

Feb. 24, 1789. Richard Lee and Anna Dodd.

Feb. 25, 1789. Thomas Lucas and Sally Garnett.

Mar. 24, 1788. William Kersey and Agnes, dau. of Charles Taylor.

Aug. 3, 1789. Reuben Jones and Patty Stevens, dau. of Mary Stower.

Dec. 24, 1788. Samuel Hill and Nancy Tate.

Feb. 7, 1788. William Herrin and Molly, dau. of William Shiflit.

Nov. 10, 1789. George Marshall Head and Milly, dau. of John and Mary Rucker.

Dec. 23, 1788. John Hamilton and Frances, dau. of William Richards.

Jan. 18, 1788. Thomas Graves and Anna, dau. of William Grady.

Feb. 7, 1788. Parke Goodall and Frankey Cox. Security Thomas Cox.

Sept. 9, 1788. Thomas Goforth and Milly Foster. Security John Foster.

Oct. 15, 1789. Joseph Griffey and Fanny Wisdom.

Dec. 19, 1789. Absalom Graves and Felicia, dau. of John White.

May 20, 1788. Laurence Gillock and Betsy Twentyman.

Dec. 27, 1788. Denny Garrell and Sally, dau. of Charles Stanton.

May 12, 1788. John Farguson and Frances, dau. of William Lucas.

Dec. 30, 1789. Reuben Dollins and Elizabeth, dau. of William Hensley.

June 2, 1789. William Deane and Sarah Boston. Security Jos. Boston.

July 27, 1789. John Davis and Mary Easten. Security Reuben Easten.

Jan. 10, 1789. Thomas Davis and Elizabeth Pannill, dau. of William.

June 29, 1789. Anselus Clarkson and Milly Jones.

Dec. 11, 1788. Lorrimer Chewning and Judith Carter.

Dec. 1, 1789. James Chishom and Catherine Raines.

Dec. 22, 1789. James Chandler and Frances, dau. of Martha McNeale.

Nov. 11, 1788. James Brown and Nancy Harrod. Security Jas. Harrod.

April 8, 1788. Robert Brooking and Patsy Russell.

July 4, 1788. William Bridges and Ann, dau. of Edumund Row.

Sept. 16, 1789. Thomas Bowler and Margaret Landrum.

Dec. 7, 1789. Ephraim Breading and Molly, dau. of Edward Franklyn.

Oct. 1, 1788. William Bolling and Phebe Hawkins Poindexter.

Nov. 5, 1788. John Bickers and Nancy Landrum.

Aug. 16, 1788. William Aery and Mary Stowers. Security Lewis Stowers.

Nov. 23, 1788. Hezekiah Atkins and Sally Chiles. Security James Chiles.

Mar. 21, 1789. William Russell and Mary Merry. Security Thomas Herndon.

(Continued.)

HENRICO COUNTY RECORDS.

Orphans' Court held at Varina, 20 August 1677. Present, Colonel William Farrar, Major William Harris, Major John Farrar, Mr. Thomas ————
An entry of the account of cattle belonging to the orphan of Robert Bradford.

An entry of the account of cattle belonging to Ann Floid in the wardship of ————

An entry of the account of cattle belonging to Anne Rowing, orphan of Henry Rowing, dec'd., in the wardship of John Watson.

An account of cattle belonging to the orphans of William Womeck, dec'd., presented by Timothy Allen, Jnr., Mary Womeck 4 cows and 1 heifer; Mary Womeck and Thomas Womeck hath between them 4 cows and 3 calves. It is consented by the Court that one of Mary Womeck's cows which is changed for a year old heifer of Abraham Womeck shall so stand confirmed.

An entry of the account of the cattle belonging to the orphans of Mr. Joseph Tanner, dec'd., in the wardship of Mr. Gilbert Platt.

An account of the estate belonging to the orphans of John Browne, dec'd., presented by John Woodson. Upon request of Sarah, wife of said John Woodson and mother to the said orphans, by and with the consent of the said John Woodson that his wife Sarah Woodson shall have in her custody and care the estate belonging to the said orphans, Mr. Abel Gower and John Clerk have entered themselves as security.

The entry of the estate of Elizabeth Taylor an orphan in the wardship of Robert Bullington.

An account of the estate of the orphans of Mr. Crawley, dec'd., viz.: John and Mary Crawley being in the wardship of Mr. Howlett.

The account of the estate of Mary Tucker, an orphan, is presented by Mr. John Pleasants.

An account of the cattle belonging to the orphans of Captain Edward Mathews, dec'd.; it is ordered that Robert Evans now guardian to the orphans of Captain Mathews do enter into bond with security, upon which Abraham Childers and William Ballowe entered on his security.

An account of the cattle belonging to John Jameson, an orphan, is presented by John Burton, Snr.

An account of the cattle of John Bowman, an orphan in the wardship of John Benson, Snr. (Burton ?)

An account ———— orphans of ———— Hudson, dec'd., presented by————, one cow ———— William Hudson, one cow and calf ————.

An account of the orphans of Morgan Peirse, dec'd., and William Peirse, dec'd.,———— viz.: William Peirse, 2 cows and 1 calf, in all 3. Francis Peirse, 3 cows and one calf, being the whole ———— of said orphans.

Account of cattle and horses belonging to the orphans of Mr. William Branch, dec'd., and Mr. Baugh, dec'd., presented by Mr. Abel Gower, viz.: in 1676 William Branch had 4 cows and 2 steer calves, and this year he hath the same and 2 steer calves increase. John Branch hath this year 1 heifer, 1 cow calf and the whole stock of these orphans is ten. Mary Baugh hath 2 young horses, 1 mare lost; Priscilla Baugh hath one mare 2 years old.

Petition of Robert Bullington against William Elam for the said Elam's putting up boundary stakes that marked the land belonging to the orphans of Francis Taylor, dec'd.

Whereas Dorothy Brady, mother to the orphans of Robert Brady, dec'd., did for their good lease unto Thomas Risby one plantation upon which said Risby was to plant an orchard, etc., which appears by condition dated 21 November, 1667.

It is ordered that William Clerk and Robert Woodson be summoned to the next Court to answer the petition of Robert Ferris, an orphan.

Ordered that Mr. Daniel Clerk having the estate and being the guardian of the orphans of Lieut. Col. Richard Cocke, dec'd., be referred for the further consideration of the Court.

Orphans' Court held at Varina, 20 August, 1678. Present, Major William Harris, Colonel Francis Epes, Lieut. Col. John Farrar, Mr. Thomas Cocke, Mr. Richard Cocke, Mr. Essex Bevill, Mr. Abel Gower.

An account of the cattle belonging to Charles and Mary Worsham, the orphans of William Worsham, dec'd., presented by Col. Francis Epes, 20 August, 1678.

An account of the cattle and mares belonging to the orphans of Morgan Peirse, dec'd., presented by John Milner for the three children, viz.: William, Francis and Elizabeth Peirse.

Account of the cattle of Robert Bradways presented by William Blackman.

Account of Ann Floyd's cattle presented by James Forrest.

Account of the stock belonging to the orphans of Richard Hudson, dec'd., viz.: Richard, Robert and William Hudson, presented by Thomas Pouldon.

Account of the stock belonging to Elizabeth Taylor, an orphan, presented by Robert Bullington.

Account of the cattle belonging to Anne Rowing, an orphan, presented by John Watson.

Account of the cattle belonging to the orphans of Mr. Joseph Tanner, presented by Mr. Gilbert Platt.

Account of stock belonging to the orphans of Mr. Crowley, dec'd., viz.: John and Mary Crowley, presented by Mr. Thomas Howlett.

Account of stock belonging to the orphans of Captain Edward Mathews, dec'd., presented by Robert Evans.

Account of the stock belonging to Mary Tucker, presented by Mr. John Pleasants.

Account of the stock belonging to the orphans of George Archer, dec'd., viz.: Elizabeth, Margery and John Archer, presented by Joseph Royall.

The Court approves of the division of the estate of Mr. Thomas Lygon, Jnr., dec'd., as presented by Mrs. Mary Lygon and distributed amongst the children, viz.: Richard, Mathew and Hugh Lygon.

Account of the stock belonging and sold for the account of the orphans of John Browne, dec'd., presented by Sarah Woodson.

Account of the cattle belonging to Mary and Thomas Womack, presented by Timothy Allen.

At an Orphans' Court held at Varina, 11 October, 1679. Present, Lieut. Colonel John Farrar, Mr. Essex Bevill, Mr. Thomas Batte, Mr. Peter Field.

Account of the cattle belonging to Thomas Bottomley, the orphan of Thomas Bottomley, dec'd., presented by Benjamin Hatcher.

Account of the cattle belonging to the orphans of Richard Hudson, dec'd., viz.: Richard, Robert and William Hudson, presented by Thos. Pouldon.

Michel Gartright hath an order granted to kill an old cow belonging to the stock of his son Samuel Gartright and to put in its place in the presence of Mr. Richard Cocke, one heifer of a year old and upwards.

Recorded the conveyance of a heifer by Bartholomew Roberts to his son Bartholomew Roberts.

Account of the stock belonging to the orphans of Morgan Peirse, dec'd., viz.: William, Francis and Elizabeth Peirse, presented by John Milner.

Account of the stock belonging to Anne and Mary Parker, orphans of William Parker, dec'd., presented by John Milner.

Account of the cattle belonging to Charles Worsham, orphan of William Worsham, presented by John Worsham in behalf of Mr. Richard Kennon.

Account of the cattle of Robert Brady, presented by William Blackman.

Account of the cattle belonging to Anne Rowing, orphan of Henry Rowing, dec'd., presented by John Watson.

Account of the cattle given to Henry Hatcher's orphans, viz.: Henry, William, Mary, Mathew, Martha and Anne Hatcher, presented by Mr. Henry Lound.

John Bowman, Jnr., and orphan in the wardship of John Bowman, Snr., being of lawful age, said John Bowman, Snr., is discharged as his guardian.

The account of Anne Floyd's cattle, presented by James Forrest.

Account of the stock belonging to John Archer, Elizabeth Archer and Margaret Archer, the orphans of George Archer, dec'd., presented by Joseph Royall.

Petition of Robert Fargus, orphan of Robert Fargus, dec'd., that he is of age and desires the estate left by his father's will recorded in Henrico, 1 October, 1669, and that Peter Ashbrooke the guardian be discharged.

Account of the cattle belonging to the orphans of Mr. Joseph Tanner, presented by Mr. Gilbert Platt.

Major William Lygon desires that a mare be recorded for the use of Martha Tanner, orphan.

(Continued.)

YORK COUNTY WILLS.

(Continued from Vol. VI, page 18.)

Heyward, Francis, 1 January, 1658; 24 August, 1659. Son Francis when he comes to the age of twenty-one; wife Mary extx.; the child my wife goes with; servant James Russell; John Bridges; brother John Heyward and Edward Mihill, overseers. Wit: John Merrey, John Bassett.

Buck, Thomas, 23 October, 1659; 17 November, 1659. Son Thomas; daughter Dorothy; Richard Smith and Nicholas Bond to be guardians of my children, also exrs. Wit: Gregory Rue, Elizabeth Fry.

Tyler, Hugh (Nuncupative will), proved 17 November, 1659. All estate to Robert Baldry.

Claxon, John, 25 August, 1659; 24 January, 1659. Cousin Thomas Hall; sister Deborah Claxon; John Harriman: Anthony Hardaker; John, son of William Ward. Wit: Anthony Hardaker, John Harriman.

Reynalls, William, ———; 24 January, 1659. Estate to wife Hannah. Wit: James Alexander, Anne Hodges.

Wheeler, Eleanor, widow, 13 April 1660; 24 April 1660. Cousins Francis and Mary Hall; Elizabeth Hooper; granddaughter Amy Harrison and her father Robert Harrison; son Nicholas Comins; John Cotton; Col. William Barber, son-in-law Robert Harrison and Nicholas Trott exrs. Wit: John Richardson, John Cotton.

Clarke, Nicholas, Snr., planter, 12 April, 1658; 24 May, 1660. Son Nicholas to have all estate and be exr. Wit: W. White, Judith Saywell.

Hodges, Augustine, (Nuncupative will), proved 24 May, 1660. Estate to my wife and my son in England, if latter be still living. Wit: John Scarsbricke, Thomas Ballard.

Whitehead, Thomas, 6 April, 1660; 24 May, 1660. Mary Rogers extx.; Thomas Bates; Mary Faulkner; Mr. Malory minister of God's word; George Faulkner; John Risley; John Diserell; Richard Smith; Anne Greene; James Rogers, brother of Mary Rogers. Wit: Richard Smith, George Thompson.

Felgate, William, 29 February, 1659; 10 September, 1660. Daughter Mary in case she comes to Va.; son William Bassett; daughter Mary Bassett; wife Mary extx.; friends Col. William Barbour and Col. John Walker overseers. Wit: Francis Haddon, Stephen Torlington, William Stubbs.

Fenne, Samuel, 9 October, 1660; 12 November, 1660. Son Samuel; daughter Sarah; Mr. Robert Burne; Thomas Ballard; James Bray; wife Dorothy; John Dickeson. Wit: John Richardson, Roger Partridge.

Jones, Richard, 2 March, 1660; 12 November, 1660. Wife and three children; son Gabriel; son Richard my plantation in Hampton parish; wife Elizabeth extx. Wit: John Hansford, Edmund Peters, William Musgrave

White, Martha, widow of William White, minister of York Parish; 4 September, 1658; 24 January, 1660. Mrs. Clarke and Mrs. Mann; my husband's two children Jeremiah and Margaret White, now living in London;

Frances Brise, orphan; Mr. Jeremiah White, minister of God; Mr. Hulett; Mr. Chant, my husband's brother; Mr. Jeremiah White and Mr. Hulett, uncles to the two orphans and to be guardians; Col. Carter of Rappahannock to be exr.; Mr. Nicholas Clarke of York and Mr. Parrott of Rappahannock, overseers. Wit: Edward Alchurch, Jeffrey Wilson.

Mihill, Edward, 11 February, 1660; 25 August, 1660. Wife Elizabeth extx.; friend Edmund Chisman and William Hay, overseers. Wit: James Maudrey, Samuel Spicer, Peter Plovier.

Heyward, John, 8 February, 1660; 24 April, 1661. Eldest son Henry; second son William; wife Margaret; daughter Eleanor; wife extx.; friends William Hay, Edward Mihill and Henry Tyler of the middle plantation to be overseers. Wit: William Whitlock, Edmond Watts.

Hanford, John, of Cheescake, 9 May, 1654; 24 August, 1661. Two oldest sons John and William; sons Thomas and Charles; daughters Elizabeth, Mary and Margaret; godson John Morley, son of my neighbor Thomas Morley; wife Elizabeth extx.; Francis Willis and Edmund Peters, overseers; Robert Jones, who is now instructor of my children. Wit: John Rowland, Enris Mackentosh, Robert Jones.

Margaretts, John, Marston Parish; 2 December, 1661; 24 January, 1661. Oldest daughter Anne; daughter Hannah; Thomas Bromfield, guardian to daughter Anne; wife admx. Wit: John Woods, Robert Cobbs.

Barron, James, 2 December, 1662; 24 October, 1662. Friend Elias Davis extr. Wit: Bennett Maddon, Jas. Russell, John Merry.

Avary, George, ———; 24 April, 1665. Son Allesher Rekoll; daughters Elizabeth, Sarah and Mary; son and Henry Lewis to be overseers. Wit: Michall Bartlett, Alexander Moore.

Albritton, Francis; 9 April, 1667; 24 April, 1667. Wife extx.; eldest son Richard; sons Francis, John and George;

daughters Elizabeth, Anne and Margaret; Thomas Allen and John Hothersall overseers. Wit: Ralph Flower, Owen Morris, Thomas Greene.

Allen, Thomas, 4 November, 1668; 7 December, 1668. Wife Bethea; Samuel Allen my brother's son; Major Robert Baldry and Capt. John Scarsbrook overseers; son Thomas Yateman; godson Peter Pearce. Wit: Edmund Woodhouse, Charles Camwell.

Atwood, Richard, 24 October, 1669; 19 November, 1669. Wife Sarah and my children in England; overseers Hugh Roy and Wm. Allen. Wit: Ralph Flower, John Luke.

Bromfield, Thomas, 15 August, 1665; 2 October, 1665. Wife Mary extx.; little daughter Anne; brother John Bromfield; godson John Tiler; Anne Johnson; Mr. Henry Tiler overseer. Wit: Daniel Wyld, Hugh Parsons.

Battaine, Ashall, 10 September, 1666; 12 November, 1666. Wife Anne; three children John, Sarah and Constant Batten; son-in-law John Dawes extr. Wit: Daniel Parke, Daniel Wyld.

Bates, John, Middletown Parish, 21 September, 1666, 24 June, 1667. Eldest daughter Anne; son George; daughter Alse Deane; John Bates my youngest son; wife Elizabeth extx. (Codicil same date.) Wit: William Winston, George Bates, William Deane.

Barber, William, Hampton Parish, 18 November, 1668; 26 July, 1669. Daughter Mary Baskervyle; granddaughters Elizabeth and Mary Baskervyle; goddaughter Mary Dennett; goddaughter Elizabeth Miles; son Thomas; wife Mary extx.; son-in-law Thomas Dennett overseer; son-in-law John Baskervyle. Wit: Matthew Collins, Sarah Collins, William Smith.

Bartlett, Michaell, Planter, 9 May, 1667; 24 March, 1670. Son Michaell; wife Mary extx.; daughter Diana Bartlett; son-in-law Alexander Moore, who married my daughter Elizabeth; son John. Wit: John Figg, Edmund Watts.

(Continued.)

NORTHAMPTON COUNTY WILLS.

Stratton, Benjamin, 29 June, 1716; 19 May, 1717. Sons Benjamin and John; grandson Benjamin Johnson; granddaughter Ann Johnson; two sons to be extrs. Wit: Richard Thorman and Dixon Knight.

Kendall, William, Jr., 11 October, 1718; 16 November, 1718. Son John; daughters Sarah, Ann Parke and Palmer Kendall; the child my wife now goes with; my sister Ann Hunt; Gauton Hunt; my sister Esther. Extx. wife Tabitha. Wit: Nicholas Powell and Francis Batson.

Rice, Henry, 6 November, 1718; 16 December, 1718. Mother Ann Rice; sister Mary Peters; wife Sarah and the child she now goes with. Extx. wife. Wit: William Kendall and Ann Wilmonth.

Firkittle, Hamon, 17 November, 1718; 16 December, 1718. Wife Frances; sons John and William; daughter Comfort. Extx. wife. Wit: Bartholomew Pettit, Thomas Goffigan, Jnr.

Harmanson, Thomas, 30 April, 1723; 14 September, 1725. Wife Elizabeth; son William; daughter Catherine; cousin John Robins; daughter Esther; William Tazewell; Mathew Harmanson; John Harmanson. Extx. wife. Wit: Gertrude Harmanson, Sophia Harmanson, Jonathan Stephens.

Ellegood, Thomas Ward, 5 September, 1724; 14 September, 1725. Wife Bridget; Capt. Ralph Pigott; son Thomas Ward Ellegood; child my wife goes with. Extx. wife. Wit: John Wilson, Smith Watts, John Fitchett.

O'Neale, Henry, 13 August, 1725; 13 October, 1725. To friend Thomas James my whole personal estate in case my son Abraham shall not come to demand the estate. Extr. Thomas James. Wit: Luke Johnson, Obedience Parramore.

Batson, Thomas, 4 November, 1725; 14 December, 1725. Son Daniel; wife Susannah; my children Mary, Allen, Peter, Susannah, Elizabeth and Thomas Batson, Jnr. Extx. wife. Wit: Wm. Willett, John Hall, Thomas Griffith.

Mapp, John, Snr., 27 October, 1725; 14 December, 1725. Sons Howson, John and Samuel; daughter Mary. Extx. wife Esther. Wit: Argoll Yardley West, Thorogood West, Samuel Bernard.

Warren, John, Snr., 18 November, 1725; 14 December, 1725. Sons Patrick, George and Henry; daughter Jane; wife Mary extx. Wit: Henry Warren, Snr., Matt. Warren, David Williams.

Wilson, James, 8 November, 1725; 14 December, 1725. Daughter Hannah; friend John Webb, Jnr., brother Thomas; extx. wife Ann. Wit: John Stratton, Thomas Wilson, Robert Warren.

Willett, William, Jnr., 13 December, 1725; 11 January, 1725. Son Thomas and daughter Mary; wife Rose extx. friends Thomas and John Goffigon to be overseers. Wit: William Willett, Ann Willett, Thos. Goffigon.

Wilkins, Argall, 2 January, 1725; 13 January, 1725. Sons John, Argall, Berry and Watkins Wilkins; son in law Joseph Warren; daughter Elizabeth Hamilton. Extx. wife Mary. Wit: Culpeper Pigott, David Dolbe, Henry Warren, Ralph Pigott.

Luker, Thomas, 24 December, 1725; 9 February 1725. Daughters Amy and Esther; sons Speakman and Thomas; wife Esther to be extx. John Waterfield and George Luker overseers. Wit: Peter Roscoe, Elizabeth Roscoe.

Blair, Barbara, 21 January, 1725; 8 December, 1725. Sons Clark and Henry; Susanna, wife of Robert Milliken; daughter Christian. Extr. Thomas James. Wit: Luke Johnson, John Roberts, Sarah Roberts.

Batson, Francis, Parish of Hungars; 22 February, 1725; 8 March, 1725. Sons Jonathan, Nehemiah and Solomon; daughters Ann and Barbara. Extx. wife Ann. Wit: John Batson, Nathl. Powell, David Williams.

Tatum, John, 4 March, 1725; 8 March, 1725. Daughter Ann Powell; children John, David, Bowker, Thomas and Winifred Tatum; wife Mary extx. Wit: Thomas Gossigon, Caesar Evans.

Watts, Thomas, Mariner; 11 March, 1725; 12 April, 1726. Eldest son John Wilkins Watts; daughters Frances and Esther; son Thomas. Extx. wife Esther. Wit: Wm. Tazewell, Katherine Robins, John Wilkins, Jnr.

Cowdry, Josias, 10 May, 1726; 14 June, 1726. Wife Charity; godson Josias Cowdry; children Thomas, Elizabeth, Grace and Joshua. Extr. son Thomas. Wit: Grace Frost, Jacob Stringer.

Wilkins, John, Planter; 16 June, 1726; 12 July, 1726. Son George; daughter Ann Mary; wife Violet and brother Argoll Wilkins, to be exrs. Wit: Culpeper Pigott, Joseph Warren, John Markland.

Hammon, Philip, 4 January, 1725; 8 November, 1726. To wife Elizabeth my entire estate. Wit: John Atkinson, John Jones.

Batson, Ralph, 16 April, 1724; 8 November, 1726. Daughters Sophia, Abigail and Amy; godson Matt. Batson; wife Abigail to be extx. Wit: Thomas Dell, John Luke, Benj. Dunton, Jnr.

Godwin, Devorax, Planter; 30 December, 1726; 14 February, 1726. Sons Joseph, William, Daniel and Devorax; my brother Daniel; daughters Mary and Susanna; daughter Ann West; my wife extx. Wit: Thomas Cable, Daniel Godwin, Margaret Cable.

Fisher, Thomas, 17 August, 1723; 12 September, 1727. To wife Sarah my entire estate. Wit: Wm. Grice, Rebecca Wilson.

Dunton, Elizabeth, 6 November, 1727; 14 November, 1727. Son Stephen; daughter Elizabeth Lingo; daughter Isabel; son John O'Deer to be extr. Wit: John Waterfield, Henry Spratling.

Mongong, Philip, 5 January, 1727; 9 January, 1727. Wife Dinah sole legatee and extx. Wit: Henry Speakman, Richard Irish.

Ellegood, Thomas, Planter ————; 13 February, 1727. To William and Josias Lowery, sons of John Lowery;

Sophia Willis; George, son of Josias Willis; Josias Willis, Jnr. Wit: Edward Rooke, Elizabeth Kite.

Willis, George, Planter; 5 February, 1727; 13 February, 1727. Brother Josias Willis; daughter Caroline Shepperd; daughter Elizabeth Willis; daughter Leah Willis; brother Wm. Willis, dec'd. Wit: Edward Rooke, William Scott.

Smith, Thomas, 14 September, 1726; 13 February, 1727. Daughter Edith; wife Ede; my children. Wit: Richard Darck, William Dunston.

Eyre, Severn, 10 February, 1727-8; 10 April, 1728. Sons Littleton and Severn; Gertrude and Henry Harmanson to be exrs. Wit: Amos Underhill; Jonathan Stott, Robert Nottingham, Henry Clegg.

Haggoman, Isaac, 16 March, 1727-8; 10 April, 1728. Son Saluonia; son John; to eldest daughters of each of my sons; sons to be exrs. Wit: Matt. Harmanson, Andrew Andrew, John Luke, John Dillon.

Fletcher, Robert, 1 March, 1727; 10 April, 1728. Sons William and Robert; wife Winifred. Wit: Cornelius Berry, Thos. Goffigon, James Goffigon.

Rabyshaw, William, 26 February, 1727; 10 April, 1728. Grandson Rabyshaw Jenkins; granddaughter Mary Jenkins; William and Robert, sons of Robert Fletcher; son in law Thomas Jenkins and my daughter Mary Jenkins. Exr. Thomas Jenkins. Wit: Hillary Stringer, George Harmanson John Clay.

Parramore, John, 11 February, 1727-8; 14 May, 1728. Daughter Mary; wife Sarah; to brother Thomas all my land in the Province of Maryland. Extx. wife. Wit: Luke Johnson, John White, Mary White.

Fitchett, Thomas, 26 January, 1727; 14 May, 1728. Sons Salathiel and Joshua; daughters Sophia and Susannah; wife Clease. Exr. Robert Trevor. Wit: John Fitchett, Edward Mills, John Trevor.

Stakey, Simon, 16 January, 1727; 14 May, 1728. Sister Sarah Layler; goddaughter Margaret Stakey. Exr. brother Wm. Stakey. Wit: George Dewey, Leah Dewey.

Warren, Argill, 4 September, 1721; 14 May, 1728. Son Matthew; daughter Mary Wilkins; son Argill; daughter Ann Esdall; son Benjamin; son Henry; daughter Elizabeth; son Robert; son John; daughter Ursly; my wife. Exr. son Robert. Wit: Philip Jacob, Nathl. Powell, Devoreaux Godwin.

Senner, John, 30 January, 1727; 14 May, 1728. Wife Martha; daughters Isabel and Mary; friends Henry Warren, Jnr., and Thomas Goffigon trustees. Wit: Wm. Bishop, Edward Peake, William Willet.

Robison, George, 8 November, 1719; 14 May, 1728. To wife Sarah entire estate. Wit: William Willett, John Williams.

Savage, Thomas, Gent., Cherry Stones; 20 August, 1726; 11 June, 1728. Son George; daughter Sophia; daughter Margaret Force and her husband James; son Thomas; daughter Mary, wife of William Copeland; granddaughter Elizabeth Copeland; daughter Sarah, wife of Francis Pugh; brother George Harmanson and coz. John Roberts. Exr. son George. Wit: Isaac Stringer, Hillary Stringer, Elishe Stringer.

Savage, George, Gent., 28 January, 1727; 11 June, 1728. Brother Thomas; sister Margaret Force; sister Sophia. Exr. brother Thomas. Wit: John Cheese, Francis Griffin, Elizabeth Savage.

White, Anne, 3 February, 1727; 11 June, 1728. Granddaughter Anne Nottingham; son in law John Marshall; Michael Nottingham; daughter Sarah Nottingham; granddaughter Elizabeth Marshall; daughter Mary Marshall. Exr. John Marshall Wit: Thomas Cable, Margt. Cable, Richard Hays.

Westerhouse, Nicholas ———; 11 June, 1728. Wife Elizabeth all my estate; Thos. Westerhouse and Andrew Andrews to overseer my children in case my wife dies. Wit: John Luke, William Roan, Isaac Scady.

EARLY SETTLERS IN VIRGINIA.

(Continued from page 17.)

Francis, John, transported by Richard Bennett, 26 June, 1635.

Francklin, Francis (servant), transported by Hannibal Fletcher in the "Revenge" in 1634.

Franklin, Henry, transported by Capt. Adam Thorogood in the "John and Dorothy" in 1634.

Freeman, Bennett, brother of Bridges Freeman of James City Co., 1 Dec., 1635.

Freeman, Bridget, wife of Bridges Freeman of James City Co., 1 Dec., 1635.

Freeman, Mill, transported by Christopher Stoakes of Elizabeth City Co., 28 July, 1635.

French, Daniel (servant), transported in 1622 by Elmer Phillips.

Fuller, Thomas, transported in the "Southampton" in 1622 by John Cheesman of Elizabeth City.

Gany, Ann (head right), wife of William Gany, Accomac, 17 Sept., 1635.

Gany, Ann (head right), daughter of William Gany, Accomac, 17 Sept., 1635.

Gany, Henry (head right), brother of William Gany, Accomac, 17 Sept., 1635.

Gany, William (head right), son of William Gany, Accomac, 17 Sept., 1635.

Gargreave, Jean, transported by George Keith, 29 July, 1635.

Garnett, John (head right), 50 acres for his first wife Alice, her son Peter Hoope, and Elizabeth his now wife, 14 Nov., 1635.

Garsell, Robert (servant), transported by John Jackson, 9 June, 1635.

Gastrock, William, transported in the "Hopewell" in 1633 by Capt. Adam Thorogood.

George, Jane, wife of John George, 7 Nov., 1635.

Gerrard, John, transported by George Keith, 29 July, 1635.

Gibson, John, transported by Christopher Branch of Henrico, 8 Dec., 1635.

Gilbert, Elizabeth, transported by Richard Bennett, 26 June, 1635.

Gaines, Martha, transported 7 Nov., 1700 by James Boughar, gent., of King and Queen county.

Gilbert, George (servant), transported by Joseph Johnson, 19 June, 1635.

Giles, Henry (servant), transported by Joseph Johnson, 19 June, 1635.

Giles, John, transported by Jeremiah Clement, 11 June, 1635.

Gill, William, transported by Thomas Baywell, 7 Nov., 1635.

Giss, John, transported by Thomas Smith, 21 July, 1635.

Glascock, Richard, transported by Richard Bennett, 26 June, 1635.

Godbeare, Hector (servant), transported by Wm. Spencer, 19 June, 1635.

Godfrye, John, transported by Thomas Harris of Henrico, 11 Nov. 1635.

Godwin, Daniel, transported by William Barker, 26 Nov., 1635.

Goodson, John, transported by William Swan, James City, 5 Nov., 1635.

Gosman, Elizabeth, transported by Capt. Adam Thorogood, in the "Christopher and Mary," 24 June, 1635.

Gouls, William, transported in the "Anne" in 1623 by Capt. William Epes of Accomac.

Grandy, John, transported by John Sparkes, 3 June, 1635.

Gray, Francis (servant), transported by Joseph Johnson, 19 June, 1625.

Gray, Thomas, son of Thomas Gray of James City, 27 Aug., 1635.

Gray, William, son of Thomas Gray of James City, 27 Aug., 1635.

Green, George, transported by George Sandys, James City, in 1624.

Greene, John, transported by Thomas Harwood, 7 July, 1635.

Gye, Gilbert, transported in the "Hopewell" in 1623 by Capt. Adam Thorogood.

Halcock, Thomas (servant), transported by William Stone of Accomac, 4 June, 1635.

Hall, Edward, transported by Thomas Harwood, 7 July, 1635.

Hall, Hugh, transported by Pharaoh Flinton of Elizabeth City in the "Margaret and John" in 1623.

Hamer, Edward, transported by Capt. William Peirce, 22 June, 1635.

Hand, Thomas (servant), transported in the "Charles" in 1621 by John Bush of Elizabeth City.

Hanwell, John, transported by Lieut. John Cheesman of Charles River Co., 21 Nov., 1635.

Harding, Mary, transported by Richard Bennett, 26 June, 1635.

Harper, Francis, transported by Hugh Cox, 6 Dec., 1634.

Harris, Henry (servant), transported by William Stone of Accomac, 4 June, 1635.

Harris, Henry, transported by Samuel Weaver, 2 July, 1635.

Harris, John, transported in the "Truelove" in 1628 by Capt. Adam Thorogood.

Harris, Thomas, transported in the "Temperance" in 1621 by Lieut. Thomas Flint.

Harris, William (servant), transported in the "George" in 1621 by William Claiborne of James City.

Harrison, James, transported by Capt. William Peirce, 22 June, 1635.

Harrison, Henry, transported by Capt. William Peirce, 22 June, 1635.

Harte, Rebecca, wife of Henry Harte, Jamestown Island, 1 Aug., 1635.

Hartwell, Henry (servant), transported by William Stone, Accomac, 4 June, 1635.

Hatton, Daniel, transported in the "Hopewell" in 1633, by Capt. Adam Thorogood.

Hatton, Jeffrey, transported by George Minifie, 2 July, 1635.

Haughton, Robert, transported by William Wilkinson, minister, 20 Nov., 1635.

Hawks, Mary, transported by William Swan, James City, 5 Nov., 1635.

Hayden, Elizabeth (servant), transported in the "London Merchant" in 1620 by Lieut. Albino Lupo, Elizabeth City.

Herring, Henry, transported by Miles Cary, gent., York Co., 7 Nov., 1700.

Hewes, John, transported by James Boughar, gent., of King and Queen Co., 7 Nov., 1700.

Hayes, Hugh (servant), transported by William Stone, Accomac, 4 June, 1635.

Hayes, John (servant), transported in the "George" in 1617 by Lieut. Albino Lupo, Elizabeth City.

Hayes, Richard, transported by Richard Bennett, 26 June, 1635.

Haynes, William, Jnr., transported by George Sandys, James City, 1624.

Hayward, Howell, transported by Capt. Thos. Willoughby, 6 Nov., 1635.

Heale, Richard, transported in the "Eleanor" in 1622 by Capt. William Tucker.

Heasoll, Robert, transported in the "Hopewell" 1628, by Capt. Adam Thorogood.

Heath, John, transported by Capt. William Peirce, 22 June, 1635.

Hedler, John (servant), transported by William Gany, Accomac, 17 Sept. 1635.

Heele, George, transported by John Parrott, 24 May, 1635.

Heutt, Richard (servant), transported by Capt. Francis Epes, 26 Aug., 1635.

Hewes, Ralph, transported by Richard Bennett, 26 June, 1635.

Heyes, Peter, transported by John Upton, 7 July, 1635.

(Continued.)

VIRGINIA REVOLUTIONARY SOLDIERS.

Guilliam, Wm., Private, Contl. Line, end of the war.

Singleton, Anthony, Captain, Contl. Line, 3 years' service.

Whitaker, Wm., Lieut., Contl. Line, end of the war.

Keith, Daniel, Private, Contl. Line, end of the war.

Stokes, Christopher, Sergeant, Contl. Line, 3 years' service.

Chapman, Jno., Sergeant, State Line, 3 years' service.

Johnson, Richard, Corporal, Contl. Line, 3 years' service.

Jones, Albridgton, Lieut., Contl. Line, 3 years' service.

Ridley, Thos., Major, Contl. Line, 3 years' service.

Tune, Wm., Sergeant, State Line, 3 years' service.

Cornelius, Josiah, Private, Contl. Line, 3 years' service.

Edwards, Edmond, Private, Contl. Line, 3 years' service.

Matthews, Benj., Private, Contl. Line, 3 years' service.

Santee, Wm., Private, State Line, 3 years' service.

Burwell, Nathl., Captain, Va. Artillery, Contl. Line, 7 years'
    service.

Waterfield, Peter, Private, Contl. Line, 3 years' service.

Johnson, Stephen, Private, Contl. Line, 3 years' service.

Maden, Robert, Private, State Line, 3 years' service.

Dixon, Anthony F., Surgeon, State Line, 3 years' service.

Bryant, John, Private, Contl. Line, 3 years' service.

Wilson, John, Private, Contl. Line, 3 years' service.

Ederman, John, Ensign, Contl. Line, 3 years' service.

Mitchell, John, Sergeant, Contl. Line, 3 years' service.

Henry, Joseph, Private, Contl. Line, 3 years' service. Jas.
    Hewey, heir at law, Dec. 16, 1783.

Lockhart, Jas., Private, Contl. Line, 3 years' service.

King, John, Private, Contl. Line, 3 years' service.

Donnakin, Saul, Private, Contl. Line, 3 years' service.

Tuggle, Joshua, Private, Contl. Line, 3 years' service.

Hudson, John, Private, State Line, 3 years' service.

Baldwin, Jas., Private, Contl. Line, 3 years' service.

Gimbo, Wm., Sergeant, Contl. Line, 3 years' service.

Payne, Jno., Private, Contl. Line, 3 years' service.

Jennings, Solomon, Sergeant, Contl. Line, 3 years' service.

Barnes, Jas., Private, Contl. Line, 3 years' service.

Knight, Andrew, Private, Contl. Line, 3 years' service.

Bradford, Hy., Sergeant, Contl. Line, 3 years' service.

Bailey, Simon, Private, Contl. Line, 3 years' service.

Eustace, Jno., Captain, Contl. Line, 3 years' service. Eustace, heir at law, Dec. 19, 1783.

Robinson, Jno., Lieut., Contl. Line, 3 years' service.

Nunnemaker, Lewis, Private, State Line, 3 years' service.

Joy, Richard, Private, Contl. Line, 3 years' service.

Heth, Wm., Colonel, Contl. Line, June, 1779, May 21, 1783.

Bowen, Jno., Jr., Contl. Line, 3 years' service.

Lewis, Jno., Private, Contl. Line, 3 years' service.

Wallerson, Robt., Corporal, Contl. Line, 3 years' service.

Gunter, Chas., Private, Contl. Line, 3 years' service.

Broek, Elias, Private, State Line, 3 years' service.

Almond, John, Sailor, State Navy, 3 years' service.

Pool, Edward, Corporal, State Line, 3 years service.

Walters, Jas., Sailor, State Navy, 3 years' service.

Davis, Jas., Private, State Line, 3 years' service.

Been, Jno., Sailor, State Navy, 3 years' service.

Jackson, Saml., Private, State Line, 3 years' service.

Gray, Geo., Private, Contl. Line, 3 years' service.

Butler, Edward, Sailor, State Navy, to end of war.

Rudd, Benj., Sailor, State Navy, 3 years' service.

Henry, Jas., Private, State Line, 3 years' service.

Johnson, Wm., Sailor, State Navy, 3 years' service.

Pierie, Thos., Private, State Line, 3 years' service.

Bennet, Wm., Private, State Line, 3 years' service.

Bully, Edwd., Boatswain, State Navy, 3 years' service.

Purcell, Robt., Private, State Line, 3 years' service.

Bruin, Peter Byan, Major, Contl. Line, 3 years' service.

Cook, Joseph, Private, Contl. Line, 3 years' service.

McCant, Jas., Private, Contl. Line, 3 years' service.

Hogins, Isham, Sergeant, Contl. Line, 3 years' service.

Dogan, Hy., Private, Contl. Line, 3 years' service.

Sampson, Spencer, Private, Contl. Line, 3 years' service.

Tasker, Jas., Private, Contl. Line, 3 years' service.

Hodgings, Saml., Private, Contl. Line, 7 years' service.

Aldridge, Jas., Private, Contl. Line, 3 years' service.

Holliday, Jas., Private, Contl. Line, 3 years' service.

Alva, Robert, Private, Contl. Line, 3 years' service.

Ralls, Nathl., Sergeant, Contl. Line, 3 years' service.
Mead, Mahlon, Private, Contl. Line, 3 years' service.
Childress, Hy., Private, Contl. Line, 3 years' service.
Ashley, Benj., Lieut., Contl. Line, 3 years' service.
Evans, John, Private, Contl. Line, 3 years' service.
Johnson, Wm., Captain, Contl. Line, 7 years' service.
Campbell, Wm., Genl, dec'd warrant to Chas. Campbell, son
　　and heir, Dec. 23, 1783.
Drew, John, Lieut., Contl. Line, end of war.
Long, Gabriel, Captain, Contl. Line, 3 years' service.
Mitchell, Geo., Sergeant, Contl. Line, 3 years' service.
Williams, Rice, Private, State Line, 3 years' service.
Powers, Wm., Private, Contl. Line, 3 years' service.
Soles, Wm., Private, Contl. Line, 3 years' service.
Shackleford, Major, Private, Contl. Line, 3 years' service.
Shackelford, Henry, Private, Contl. Line, 3 years' service.
Griffin, Thos., Jr., Private, State Line, 3 years' service.
Foster, Peter, Sailor, State Navy, 3 years' service.
Bedenger, Daniel, Lieut., Contl. Line, 3 years' service.
Nelson, Wm., Lieut.-Col., Contl. Line, 3 years' service.
Innes, Jas., Colonel, Contl. Line, 3 years' service.
Drew, Jno.. Lieut., Contl. Line, end of war.
Markham, Jas., Captain, State Navy, 7 years' service.
Morris, Isaac, Private, Contl. Line, 3 years' service.
Dupree, Wm., Private, Contl. Line, 3 years' service.
Mercer, Jno. F., Captain, Contl. Line, 3 years' service.
Marshall, Jno., Boatswain, State Navy, 3 years' service.
Buns, Jno., Private, State Line, 3 years' service.
Walters, Richard, Capt.-Lieut., Contl. Artillery, 7 years' service.
Carnes, Patk., Captain, Contl. Line, 3 years' service.
Mooney, Isaac, Private, Contl. Line, 3 years' service.
Petrie, Alex, Sergeant, Contl. Line, 3 years' service.
Galloway, Terrey, Private, Contl. Line, 3 years' service.
Bernard, Thos., Corporal, Contl. Line, 3 years' service.
Slaughter, Nathl., Private, Contl. Line, 3 years' service.　Jno.
　　Slaughter, heir at law, Jan. 12, 1784.
Boyd, Jas., Private, Contl. Line, 3 years' service.

Bolling, Jesse, Private, Contl. Line, 3 years' service.

Robinson, Jas., Corporal, Contl. Line, 3 years' service.

Farmer, Jesse, Private, Contl. Line, 3 years' service.

Pediford, Edward, Private, Contl. Line, 3 years' service.

Richardson, Robert, Private, Contl. Line, 3 years' service.

Anderson, Nathl., Lieut., Contl. Line, 3 years' service.

Nelson, John, Captain, Contl. Line, 3 years' service.

Anderson, Wm., Sergeant, Contl. Line, 3 years' service (original voucher says Wm. Andrews).

Alford, Jacob, Private, Contl. Line, 3 years' service.

Carrington, Clement, Ensign, Contl. Line, 3 years' service.

Coleman, Richard, Captain, Contl. Line, 3 years' service.

Hunt, Samuel, Private, Contl. Line, 7 years' service.

Roney, John, Lieut., Contl. Line, 7 years' service.

Bundy, Francis, Private, Contl. Line, end of war.

Meals, Samuel, Seaman, State Navy, 3 years' service.

Rickman, Wm., Dr., Director-General Contl. Line, 3 years' service. Warrant to widow Eliz. Rickman, Jan. 13, 1784.

COLLEGE OF ARMS OF CANADA.

By Edict of King Louis XIV. in 1664: Confirmed by Royal
Commission of the Appeal of Malta of 1877.

*Under Council of the Aryan and Seigneurial Order of the
Empire in America.*

MEMORANDA.

I.

This College of Arms is the Official Court of Heraldic
Registry of America, wherein armigerous right and rank are
established and where symbols are added to the arms of those
proven under seal, that the true may be known from the false.

On account of the prevalence of fraud in American ancestry and arms, no claims of distinction thereby are accepted
anywhere unless the titles by which they are held are guaran-
teed by the Heraldic Court of the College of Arms. Costly books
on "Famous Families of America" have thus become so worthless by the admixture of the false with the presumably genuine,
that their arms and rank are unworthy of notice, and if borne
without warrant, are reckoned, in England and America, to be
warrantless through inability to obtain the seal of the Commissioners of the Heraldic Court and the symbol of authentication of the College of Arms.

II.

No Heraldic Court will certify to descent from armigerous
ancestry unless probative proof is given. Circumstantial evi-

dence of bearing the same name and tradition of origin in the same locality, with official, gentry and proprietory condition in every generation of the family chain, are deemed worthy to give right to bear the same arms, but with a symbol of difference to show that the right, though conceded, is circumstantial rather than documentary.

In like manner, the College of Arms of Canada follows the same law by regarding the *condition* of the *First American Ancestor* as the *criterion* of his *parental condition in Europe* in the acknowledgment of traditionary and circumstantial armigerous descent and rank.

MARKS OF AUTHENTICATION.

I.

Families of the Baronets of Nova Scotia (signed for by the Earl of Galloway in 1908; of the Seigneurs of the Empire (represented by the Duke of Veragua); of the Bannerets of Quebec (represented by the Baroness Dorchester, who founded the Dorchester decoration of the order); of the Seigneurs of Canada and Louisiana (represented by the Baron de Longueuil); of the Manorial and Titular Grantees of America (represented by the Brents of Maryland, next of kin to Lord Baltimore); of the Equestors of the Yellow Rose, Knights of the Golden Horseshoe of Virginia; of the Royal and Military Order of the Mountain Eagle, etc.—all confederated in the Aryan and Seigneurial Order—are granted a special coronet over the arms, and are eligible to the Dorchester Decoration of the Empire in the male line, family name of any of the above distinctions. So are those holding matriculation papers from the Heraldic Courts of the Seigneurial Nobility of Europe.

II.

First Ancestor to America before 1783, who used armorial seal or who was put on the list for Royal Provincial Council by order of the King, gives Consular rank to his family; to whose registered descendants of family name the Court decrees *the Consular Button* of rank, with *azure octofoil* added to recorded arms.

III.

First Ancestor to America before 1783, who was a landed proprietor and military or civil officer, gives Burgess rank with the button, and red octofoil to such arms as circumstantial evidence before the College decides.

IV.

First Ancestor to America after 1783, who was a man of property and station, and acknowledged by signed and sealed letters of an armigerous family of Europe, duly recorded there to be one of themselves, gives to his registered descendants of the name, the button of Alumnal rank, and the green octofoil of authentication is added to their registered arms.

V.

Those receiving the Button and Diploma of the Heraldic Court of the College of Arms are armigers of the same, ranked with the Armigerous Nobility of Europe by international treaties of comity. Armigers of 16 quarterings are admitted to the Seigneurial Order and Decoration.

COURT DRESS.

The Seigneurial Order has its own Dress and Decoration of the Empire. The Armigers wear the conventional black dress, but with gilt buttons and epaulettes; dress sword; blue, red or green sash, rosette and button of Consular, Burgess or Alumnal Degree; black felt hat with gilt band; blue, red or green feather.

THE BARONETS OF NOVA SCOTIA.

Their Family History and Armorial Bearings.

From the Archives of the College of Arms of Canada.

In 1611 all the country from Lund Island to the St. Lawrence had been ceded by King James to William Alexander, Earl of Sterling, who was created a Viscount of Canada. The land was divided into feudal fiefs called Baronetcies, the titles of which were conferred on these gentlemen of armigerous race who contributed one thousand pounds each, and who agreed on being invested with the title of Baronet, to occupy the fief in that Province and to sit in the Council of the same as a magistrate.

In 1632, what part of this grant had not been occupied by democratic Puritans, was ceded to France by the treaty of Breda (Acadia), and did not become again the property of the British Crown until 1713 by the treaty of Utrecht. Between 1632 and 1703 (when the last title of Baronet of Nova Scotia had been granted by Queen Ann, the last of the Stuart sovereigns), more than 125 Baronetcies had been created; but while their descendants bear the title of Baronet to-day in Britain, they are not fully and legally possessed of the same until they perform their duty in registering in Canada, according to the terms of the Charter of creation of the Baronets of Nova Scotia. On their registration in the College of Arms of Canada, they are at once eligible to the Council or Senate, with other Seigneurial and armigerous noblesse, and by special concession place over their shield a coronet of thistles alternating with eight balls argent, five being seen in front when emblazoned with the arms.

The following are those families whose historical outlines have been collected.

MACKAY OF FAR.

Sir Donald Mackay of Far was made a Baronet of Nova Scotia in 1627, and elevated to the peerage as Baron Reay in

1628. His wife was Barbara, daughter of Kenneth Mackenzie, Baron Kintail. From him amongst his other descendants who bear right to the Order and the present title was Lieut.-General Alexander Mackay, Commander-in-Chief in Scotland in 1780. The family descend from Ode Mackay, who obtained extensive territorial grants in Caithness and Sutherland in 1499 and 1507. He was killed in the battle of Flodden and was succeeded by his son Donald, a very valiant and able military commander, from whom came in the fifth generation the first Baronet of Nova Scotia.

Arms.—Azure, on a chevron between three bears' heads couped argent, muzzled gules, a roebuck's head erased, between two hands issuant from the ends of the chevron, each holding a dagger ppr.

Crest.—A dexter arm from the elbow, erect, holding a dagger in pale ppr., pommel and hilt or.

Motto.—"Manu forti." Seigneurial coronet under a Baronial one.

ELPHINSTONE OF LOGIE.

Sir James Elphinstone of Logie, Baronet of Nova Scotia, 2 Dec., 1701.

Sir John, 4th Baronet died in 1743. His heiress married General Robert Dalrymple.

Arms.—Argent, on a chevron sable, between three bears' heads, erased gules, an episcopal mitre of the first, all within a bordure gules.

Crest.—A dexter hand holding a writing pen full feathered ppr.

Motto.—"Sedulitate." Seigneurial coronet.

ACHESON OF GOSFORD.

Archibald Acheson of Gosford was made a Baronet of Nova Scotia in 1628. He was Solicitor-General and Secretary of State for Scotland. From him descended Sir Archibald.

who was elevated to the peerage of Ireland where his family held lands, as Baron Gosford of County Armagh (1776), and Viscount Gosford (1785). His son Arthur was created Earl of Gosford in 1806, from whom descends the present possessor of all these titles.

Arms.—Argent, an eagle displayed with two heads, sable; beaked and membered or.

Crest.—A cock gules standing on a.trumpet or.

Motto.—"Vigilantibus." Seigneurial coronet beneath an Earl's coronet.

ATCHISON OF GLENCAIRNE.

Sir Archibald Atchison of Glencairne was made a Baronet of Nova Scotia, January 1, 1628. The Atchisons of Mounteagle and the Earl of Gosford were of the same ancestry as of Glencairne.

Arms.—Gules, an eagle displayed with two heads, sable, beaked and membered or; on a chief vert, two mullets of the field.

Crest.—A cock gules on a trumpet or. Seigneurial coronet.

OGILVY OF INVERQUHARTY.

Sir John Ogilvy of Inverquharty was made a Baronet of Nova Scotia in 1626. His wife was Ann, daughter of Sir Alexander Irvine of Drum. This family, like most of those noble families of Scotland that held honour dearer than lands and treasure and as the fount of their nobility, was legitimist in 1715 and in 1745. From him through illustrious and honorable generations is descended the present Baronet of Nova Scotia, Sir Reginald Ogilvy, Hon. Colonel of the Forfar and Kincardine Artillery.

The family traces its origin to the ancient Mormaers of Angus, one of the seven great hereditary chiefs of Scotland, who in the XI century were granted the feudal designation of Earl on the introduction of the Franco-Norman feudality into Scotland. Gilibride, Earl of Angus, tempo. David I had three sons, one of whom Gilbert assumed the name of Ogilvy from the lands which he held in 1172. From him besides the Baronets of Nova Scotia descend the Earls of Airlie.

Arms.—Quarterly: 1st and 4th, argent, a lion pass. gard., gules, gorged with an open crown, and crowned with a close imperial one, or, for OGILVY; 2nd and 3rd, argent, an eagle displayed, sable, beaked and membered gules for RAMSAY.

Crest.—A demi-lion rampant gules, armed azure. Seigneurial Coronet.

OGILVIE OF BANFF.

Sir James Ogilvie of Banff, Baronet of Nova Scotia, 30 July, 1627.

Lord Banff bore the title in 1800.

Arms.—As Ogilvie of Carnousie.

Crest.—A lion's head, erased gules.

Supporters.—Dexter, a man in armor with target ppr.; sinister, a lion gules.

Motto.—"Fideliter."

OGILVIE OF CARNOUSIE.

Sir George Ogilvie of Carnousie, Baronet of Nova Scotia, 24 Sept, 1626. Of the family of Lord Banff.

Arms.—Quarterly: 1st and 4th., argent, a lion passant gardant gules, imperially crowned or; 2nd and 3rd., argent, three papingoes vert, beaked and membered gules.

Crest.—A lion's head, erased gules.

NICOLSON OF LASWADE.

Sir John Nicolson of Laswade, Baronet of Nova Scotia, 27 July 1629. Sir Arthur, 7th Baronet was living in 1828.

Arms.—Or, three falcons' heads, erased gules, beaked argent.

Crest.—A demi-lion or.
Supporters.—Two eagles or, armed gules.
Motto.—"Generositate."

NICOLSON OF CARNOCK.

Sir Thomas Nicolson of Carnock, Baronet of Nova Scotia. Various origins have been claimed for this family. Some believe that in the Franco-Norman period they came into Scotland from England; others that they derive their descent from MacNichol, a Highland chief. At any rate, they have been among the noblesse of Scotland as far back in feudal times as most of the great families.

Arms.—Or, a lion's head between three falcons' heads, erased gules; a bordure of the last. Seigneurial Coronet.

LEVINGSTON, EARL OF NEWBURG.

Sir John Levingston, a stanch Cavalier of King Charles I was made a Baronet of Nova Scotia in 1626. His son James, was elevated to the peerage of Scotland as Viscount Newburgh in 1647. For his self sacrifice and devotion to the principles of the constitution and monarchy during the Puritan usurpation he was made Earl of Newburgh by King Charles II in 1660. He married 1st, Catherine, daughter of Theophilus Howard, Earl of Suffolk; 2nly, Anne, daughter of Sir Henry Poole, Her son Charles had a daughter and heir who married in 1724, Charles Radcliffe, 4th Earl of Derwentwater, which family gave such heroic testimony to its grandeur of soul by its noble sacrifice for the cause of legitimacy in 1715 and 1745. The Radcliffe family, which was of Franco-Norman origin, inherited the Baronetcy of Nova Scotia, from whenc it passed to the next heir Lady Ann Clifford, whose only child the Countess Cecelia married in 1757, Benedict, 5th Prince Giustiniani unto whose descendant this title of Baronet of Nova Scotia as well as that of Earl of Newburgh has passed.

The Levingstons descend from a noble of North England who in 1070 came into Scotland and founded the Leving estate, called Leving's-Town. From him descended Sir John Levingston of Kinnaird, the 1st Baronet, a younger branch of the family of Sir John of Callendar, who was also ancestor of the Earls of Callendar and Linlithgow.

Arms.—Quarterly: 1st, bendy of six argent and gules, on a chief of the last a cross of the first, for BANDINI; 2nd, gules, a tower, ppr., on a chief or, an eagle displayed sable for GIUSTINIANI; 3rd, or, a lion rampant sable for MAHONY; 4th, chequy or and azure a fesse gules for CLIFFORD; 5th, argent on a bend gules between three gilliflowers slipped ppr., two and one, an anchor of the field, all within a tressure flory-counter-flory, vert for LEVINGSTON; 6th, gules, on a bend argent, a grasshopper ppr., for GRILLO, DUKE OF MONTDRAGONE.

Seigneurial Coronet beneath a princely one.

DUNBAR, BANNERET OF QUEBEC.

William Dunbar, was a Major beneath the Royal Standard in the War of 1775-83 in North America, and by the Loyalist Act of 1789 of Quebec was entitled to an hereditary mark of Honour with the other military and civil officers who "joined the Royal Standard before the Treaty of Separation of 1783." This "mark of Honour" was determined by the Aryan and Seigneurial Order to be "Banneret of Quebec of the United Empire." He was son of Sir George Dunbar, Baronet of Nova Scotia of the Dunbars of Mochrum. He married in Canada, a daughter of the Count de Chambaud, and had two daughters, Mariel, who married George Selby, M. D., of Montreal, in whose line the title descends, and Jessy, married to Ralph Henry de La Bruyere of the Royal Engineers in Canada.

Arms.—Same as of Dunbar of Mochrum.

LIVINGSTON OF DUNNYPACE.

Sir David Livingston of Dunnypace, Baronet of Nova Scotia, 30 May, 1625. The last to bear this title was Admiral Sir Thomas Livingston, 1843.

Arms.—Argent, three cinquefoils within a double tressure flory counter-flory gules.

LIVINGSTON OF KINNAIRD.

Sir John Livingston of Kinnaird, Baronet of Nova Scotia, 29 June, 1627, afterwards Viscount Kinnaird. His grandson was Charles, 2nd Earl of Newburgh, died 1694.

Arms.—Argent on a bend between three gilliflowers gules, an anchor of the first, a double tressure flory counter-flory vert.

Crest.—A Moor's head couped ppr. banded gules and argent with pendants argent at his ears.

Supporters.—Dexter, a savage wreathed head and middle with laurel ppr.; sinister, a horse argent furnished gules.

Motto.—"Si je puis."

LIVINGSTON OF CALLENDAR.

Sir Alexander Livingston, Baronet of Nova Scotia, 20 July, 1685. He was son of the Earl of Callendar.

Arms.—Quarterly 1st and 4th for LIVINGSTON; 2nd and 3rd, sable, a bend between six billets or, for CALLENDAR.

Crest.—A dexter hand holding a sword, ppr.

Motto.—"Et domi et foris."

ELLIOT, EARL OF MINTO.

Gilbert Elliot of Stobs, was made a Baronet of Nova Scotia, 19 April, 1700. He was a Lord of Sessions with the title of Lord Minto. His son and successor Sir Gilbert had among other issue Andrew Elliot, Royal Lieutenant-Governor of the Province of New York. His eldest son, Sir Gilbert, 3rd Baronet, married the heiress Agnes-Murray Kynynmound of Melgund. His son the 4th Baronet was Viceroy of Corsica up to 1797, Baron Minto and Governor-General of Bengal and Earl of Minto in 1813, from whom descended the present Baronet and Earl who is Viceroy of India, having been the radical-liberal appointee to that position as well as to a former one of Governor-General of Canada, whose term of office was sullied by extreme subserviency to parliamentary radicals in signing the recall of the King's Commander, Lord Dundonald, at their clamerous instance, and thus ignorantly lowering the prestige of the office which he held, at least, as nominal representative of the King.

The family of Elliot originated on the borders between England and Scotland, and had obtained some renown in the border frays pro and con with the ebb and flow of what fortune might bid for in the wars of the two countries in the ancient days of their separate nationalities.

Arms.—Quarterly: 1st and 4th grand quarters, quarterly 1st and 4th, argent a bugle-horn sable, stringed and garnished gules; on a chief azure, three mullets of the first for MURRAY; 2nd and 3rd, azure, a chevron argent, between three fleurs-de-lis or, for KYNYNMOUND; 2nd and 3rd grand quarters, gules on a bend engrailed or, a baton azure, within a bordure vair for ELLIOT; over all a chief of augmentation argent; charged with a Moor's head, couped in profile, ppr., being the arms of Corsica.

Crest.—A dexter arm embowed, issuant from the clouds, throwing a dart, all ppr.

Motto.—"Suaviter et fortiter." Seigneurial Coronet under an Earl's.

ELLIOT OF HEADSHAW.

Sir Gilbert Elliot of Headshaw, Baronet of Nova Scotia, 19 April, 1700.

Arms.—Gules, on a bend engrailed or, a baton azure, within a bordure vair.

Crest.—A dexter hand issuant of a cloud, throwing a dart, ppr.

Motto.—"Non eget arcu." Seigneurial Coronet.

ERSKINE, EARL OF MAR AND KELLIE.

Sir Charles Erskine of Cambo was made a Baronet of Nova Scotia, in 1666. He was Lyon King of Arms of Scotland. His father was Sir Thomas Erskine of Gogar, Earl of Kellie, whose father, the 5th Lord Erskine was Guardian of

King James VI and Governor of Stirling Castle. Sir Alexander, the 2nd Baronet was also Lyon King of Arms for Scotland 1681. His wife was a cousin, Ann Erskine, daughter of Alexander, 3rd Earl of Kellie. Sir Charles Erskine, 6th Baronet of Nova Scotia, on the extinction of the direct line of the Earls of Kellie succeeded as the 8th Earl in 1795, and on his death, unmarried in 1799, his uncle, Thomas, son of Sir Charles the 6th Baronet, succeeded as 9th Earl of Kellie, since which time the succession has been direct to the present day.

The family of Erskine, probably Franco-Norman like most of the feudal aristocracy, took their name from the lands of Erskine on the Clyde, which they held in feudal tenure as early as the days of King Alexander II. Henry de Erskine was Baron in 1220. From him came Sir Robert de Erskine, Grand Chamberlain of Scotland 1356, and Constable of Sterling Castle after 1368. From him came Sir Robert who was Earl of Mar in 1438, and from him came John, Earl of Mar, Secretary of State for Scotland in 1706, who raised the Standard for legitimacy and the Stuarts in 1715. He was granted the title of Duke of Mar with the parchment to sign of the Marquisate of Garioch by King James VII, the latter title of which he bestowed on his relative John Erskine de Mar, who, on the failure of the Cause fled to America and landed at Kittery on the coast of New England in 1719, with whose posterity the legitimist title rests.

Arms.—Quarterly: 1st and 4th, argent a pale sable for ERSKINE; 2nd and 3rd, a bend between six crosses-crosslet fitchee for MAR; over all a shield gules, thereon the Royal Crown of Scotland within a double-tressure flory-counter-flory or.

Crests.—A hand holding a dagger ppr. for ERSKINE; another with a dem; lion gules, armed argent for KELLIE.

Mottoes.—"Je pense plus" for ERSKINE, 2nd "Decori decus addit avite" for KELLIE. Seigneurial Coronet under an Earl's Coronet.

ERSKINE, EARL OF ROSSLYN.

Charles Erskine of Alva, was made a Baronet of Nova Scotia, 30 April, 1666. His father was Sir Charles of Alva, 4th son of John Erskine, Earl of Mar, K.G., Treasurer of Scotland, by his marriage with Mary, daughter of Esme Stewart, 1st Duke of Lenox. His descendant, Sir James St. Clair Erskine inherited the Earldom of Rosslyn by the death of his maternal uncle, Alexander Wedderburn, Lord High Chancellor of Gt. Britain, who was the 1st Earl of that name. The present Earl and Baronet as well as younger lines in America are descended from this bearer of the title. A sketch of the family has been given elsewhere.

Arms.—Quarterly: 1st, argent, a cross engrailed sable for St. Clair; 2nd, argent, a pale sable for Erskine; 3rd, azure, a bend between six crosses-crosslets fitchee or, for Mar; 4th, argent on a chevron gules, between three roses of the last barbed vert, a fleur-de-lys of the field for difference, for Wedderburn.

Motto.—"Fight." Seigneurial Coronet beneath an Earl's.

GRANT, EARL OF SEAFIELD.

Sir Ludovico Grant succeeded to the Baronetcy of his uncle Colquhoun, Baronet of Nova Scotia (which was conferred in 1625), in 1704. He married Margaret, daughter of James Ogilvie, Earl of Seafield and Findlater, and his posterity on the extinction of the Ogilvie name succeeded to that title, while holding the Colquhoun title of Baronet of Nova Scotia, but there are younger lines of Grant in America, who are entitled through this line to enrollment in the Aryan and Seigneurial Order. The family of Grant has been given under the Barony and Seigneurie of Longueuil in these papers.

Arms.—Quarterly: 1st and 4th grand quarters, quarterly, 1st and 4th, argent, a lion passant guardant gules imperially crowned ppr. for Ogilvie; 2nd and 3rd, argent a cross engrailed sable for St. Clair; 2nd and 3rd, gules three antique crowns or for Grant.

Seigneurial Coronet beneath an Earl's.

(Continued.)

LIST OF SEIGNEURIES AND SEIGNEURS IN ARCHIVES OF COL-
LEGE OF ARMS OF CANADA, LOUISIANA AND ACADIA,
FROM REPORTS OF INTENDANTS, AND PARISH
RECORDS, COLLEGE OF ARMS OF CANADA.

A.

Jean P. d'Abbadie, Baron de St. Castin (1650).
Fabio Albergatti, Marquis de Vezza (1757).
Claude Amyot, Seigneur de Vincelette (1663).
Charles J. Amyot, Sieur du Cap St. Ignace (1691).
Gabriel G. Amiot, Sieur de Hautemenay (1791).
Jacques Arrivé, Sieur de Cormiers (1663).
Gaspard Adhémar, Seigneur de Lantagnac (1720).
Pierre André, Sieur de Ligne (1690).
Bertrand Arnault, noble (1685).
Jean Arnault, noble (1685).
René Artault, Sieur de La Tour (1663).
Louis Audet, Sieur de Bayeul (1702).
Charles J. d'Ailleboust, Sieur des Musseux (1663).
Pierre d'Ailleboust, Sieur d'Argenteuil (1669).
Nicolas d'Ailleboust, Sieur de Menteth (1700).
Paul d'Ailleboust, Sieur de Périgny (1700).
Paul d'Ailleboust, Sieur de Luis (1727).
Philippe d'Ailleboust, Sieur de Cerry (1735).
Charles Aubert, Sieur de la Chesnay (1663).
Pierre Aubert, Seigneur de Gaspé (1740).
Jacques Aubert, noble (1665).
Martin d'Aprendistigué, Sieur de Martignan (1663).
Louis Artus, Seigneur de Sailly (1663).
Michel M. Avice, Seigneur de la Garde (1755).

B.

Jacques René de Brisay, Marquis de Denonville (1685).
François de Bosche, Marquis de Beauharnois (1704).
Jean F. Bélanger, Seigneur de Bonsecours (1671).
Lois F. Bélanger, Seigneur de l'Isle (1682).
Joseph Benard, Sieur de Lavignon (1672).
Joseph Blondeau, Seigneur de la Rivière du Loup (1681).

Julien Bloys, Sieur de Sérigny (1665).

Jean Bouchart, Seigneur de Champagny (1663).

Jean Bouillet, Seigneur de la Chassaigne (1702).

Claude Bouillet, Seigneur de Chevelet (1742).

Pierre Boulanger, Seigneur de St. Pierre (1686).

Elie Bourbant, Sieur de la Bissonnière (1663).

Jean Bourdon, Seigneur de Dombourg-Neuville (1663).

Médéric Bourduceau, Sieur de la Bouchardière (1663).

Barthélémy Bourgonnière, Sieur de Hauteville (1696).

Martin Boutet, Sieur de St. Martin (1700).

Jacques Brisset, Sieur de Courchêne (1663).

J. Courchêne Brisset, Sieur de l'Ile-Dupas (1674).

Melchior Brisset, Sieur de Beaupré (1726).

Claude M. de Bégin, Chevalier (1718).

Jean B. Bernier, Sieur de St. Joseph (1734).

Alex. Berthier, Seigneur de Villemar (1702).

Charles P. Blaiz, Sieur de La Faraudière (1760).

Gilbert C. Boucoult, Sieur de La Godefuz (1730).

Thomas Jacques Baby, noble (1696).

Charles Barbel, Sieur d'Argentenay (1700).

Pierre Bécart, Sieur de Granville (1702).

Claud de Berman, Sieur de la Martinière (1664).

François Bissot, Sieur de la Rivière (1664).

Jean B. Bissot, Sieur de Vincennes (1663).

Charles F. Bissot, Sieur du Cap St. Cloud (1698).

Pierre Boucher, Seigneur de Boucherville (1663).

René J. Boucher, Seigneur de Montbrun (1729).

Lambert Boucher, Sieur de Grandpré (1693).

Ignace Boucher, Sieur de Grosbois (1698).

Jean B. Boucher, Sieur de Niverville-Chambly (1710).

Joseph Boucher, Sieur de la Broquerie (1730).

Joseph Boucher, Sieur Des Bois (1729).

Pierre L. Boucher, Seigneur de Montizambert (1759).

Jean P. Bachois, Sieur de Barrante (1755).

François Barrette, Sieur de Cormiers (1703).

Michel H. Beausacque, Sieur de Bouillemont (1729).

Antoine F. Benoit, Chevalier (1753).

Jean F. Benoit, Sieur de Courville (1789).

Joseph Bernard Carignan, Sieur de Lavignon (1689).

Pierre Boisseau, Seigneur de Bellevue (1670).

Jacques H. Bouchel, Seigneur de Courceval (1768).

Joseph Brassard-Duchesneux, Seigneur de Neuville (1747).

C.

Michel Chartier, Marquis de Lotbinière (1784).

Gaspard Chaussegros, Vicomte de Léry (1682).

Gaspard G. Chaussegros, Seigneur de la Belleplaine (1753).

Jacques Caitleau, Sieur de Champfleury (1664).

N. de Cellies, Sieur de Marbrelle (1713).

Philippe de Carion, Sieur de Fresnoy (1671).

Gabriel Celie-Duclos, Sieur du Sailly (1663).

Jean Céléron, Sieur de Blainville (1670).

J. Céléron, Chevalier (1724).

Claude Charron, Sieur de la Barre (1663).

François de Chateauneuf, Sieur de Montel (1693).

Bertrand Chesnay de la Garenne, Seigneur de Lothainville (1663).

Jacques N. Chevalier, Sieur de Beauchemin (1687).

Jean B. Chevalier, Sieur de La Durantaye (1783).

Jean B. Coté, Seigneur de l'Ile-Verte (1624).

Nicolas A. Coulon, Sieur de Villiers (1671).

Joseph Coulon, Sieur de Jumonville (1745).

Cylas Coureault, Sieur de La Coste (1689).

Michel Cressé, Sieur de la Rivière Nicolet (1680).

Aimable J. Came, Seigneur de St. Aigne (1749).

Daniel Chabert-de-Joncaire, noble (1757).

Etienne Charet, Sieur de Lauzon (1782).

Antoine Chatelain, Sieur de Dérigny (1772).

François J. Crugnet, Sieur de St. Etienne (1760).

Pierre Chicorne, Sieur de Bellevue (1670).

Fr. Chorel-Dorvilliers, Sieur de St. Romain (1663).

Médard Chouart, Sieur des Groseillers (1663).

Jacques Cochon, Seigneur de la Grande Rivière (1692).

Hughes Cochon, Seigneur de Floridore (1684).

Louis Couillard, Sieur de l'Espinay (1663).
Charles J. Couillard, Sieur des Ilets (1668).
Louis Couillard, Sieur de St. Thomas (1680).
Jean B. Couillard, Seigneur de la Rivière du Sud (1754).
Christophe Crevier, Sieur de St. Mesle (1663).
Jean Crevier, Sieur du Vernet (1680).
Nicolas Crevier, Sieur de Bellerive (1681).
Joseph Crevier, Sieur de St. François (1724).
René J. Chorel, Sieur de Dorvilliers (1714).

D.

Charles J. Douglas, Comte de Douglas (1767).
Jacques Douglas, Chevalier de Bassagnac (1760).
Nicolas Denys, Seigneur (1676).
Simon Denys, Seigneur de la Trinité (1663).
Pierre Denys, Seigneur de la Ronde (1740).
Guillaume Dagnaux, Sieur de La Motte (1742).
Simon P. Denys, Chevalier, Seigneur de Bonnaventure
(1689).
François P. Denys, Sieur de La Thibaudière (1762).
Charles P. Denys, Sieur de Vitré (1668).
Paul Denys, Sieur de St. Simon (1670).
Claude Drouet, Sieur de Richardville (1687).
Messire Sidrac Dugué, Sieur de Boisbriant (1667).
Guillemat Duplessis, Seigneur (1663).
Paul Dupuy, Sieur de l'Ile-aux-Oies (1668).
François Duval, Seigneur Duponthaut (1692).
Michel Dagneaux, Sieur de Dauval (1688).
Louis C. Dagnaux, Sieur de Quinde (1663).
François J. Delorimier, Sieur de Verneuil (1770).
Paul Derivon, Sieur de Budeumont (1715).
Bernard A. Deschevets, Sieur de Rochmont (1705).
G. Dubois, Sieur de Beaucourt (1715).
J. Dufrênel, Sieur de la Pepardière (1700).
J. Dubord, Sieur de Chaumont (1760).
Pierre Dandonneau, Marquis du Sablé (1663).
Louis Dandonneau, Sieur de l'Ile Dupas (1684).
Jean de Doubet, Sieur de la Rivière (1688).

Jean Deparrat, noble (1663).
Pierre Descayrac, Sieur de Réau (1687).
J. B. T. Deschamps, Sieur de la Bouteillerie (1680).
Joseph Desjordy, Sieur de Cabanac (1700).
François Desjordy, Sieur de St.-George (1700).
Jean Daniau, Sieur de Loney (1664).
Christophe Dufros, Sieur de La Gamerie (1701).
Jacques Dumesnil-Heurry, Sieur de St. Marc (1670).
Nicolas Dupont, Sieur de Neuville (1670).
Paul Duguet, Sieur de La Chênay (1666).
Philippe C. Duvault, Sieur de Valerenne (1687).
J. B. A. Dalciat, Sieur de la Fayolle (1768).
J. Desguires-Desrosiers, Sieur de la Rivière St. David
(1744).
Jacques P. David, Sieur de St. Eloi (1771).
René Denom, Sieur du Port-Daniel (1720).
Benj. J. Dorvilliers, Sieur de La Boiserie (1710).
Pierre de Desguerrois, Sieur des Rosiers (1724).
J. Dubouchet, Sieur de L'Hermitage (1765).
P. Dupré, Sieur de la Rivière du Loup (1685).
Antoine Duverger, Sieur d'Aubusson (1690).

E.

P. Escean, Seigneur de Berry (1670).
G. Enaud, Seigneur d'Absnobou (1670).
F. Eury, Sieur de La Perelle (1725).
Jean C. d'Estimauville, Baron de Beaumouchel (1750).

F.

Louis Faucher, Seigneur de St.-Maurice (1680).
J. Frérot, Sieur de Longval (1725).
P. Fournier, Sieur de Belleval (1785).
Pierre Ferré, Sieur de St. Charles (1659).
R. C. Fezeret, Sieur d'Oumaska (1680).
R. M. Fromanteau, Sieur de Maskinongé (1790).

(Continued.)

VOL. IX. (Old Series)
VOL. I. (New Series)   YEAR 1911   Part 4

Virginia
County Records

AND

Heraldic Quarterly Register

OF

THE UNITED STATES AND CANADA

Official Publication of the College of Arms of Canada

EDITED BY

William Armstrong Crozier, F. R. S., F. G. S. A.

The Genealogical Association, Publishers
Hasbrouck Heights
New Jersey

NOTICE TO SUBSCRIBERS.

The Virginia County Records Quarterly Magazine has been designated as the Official Publication of the College of Arms of Canada, and henceforth will be known as the "Virginia County Records and Heraldic Quarterly Register" of the United States and Canada. The volume for 1911 being the first volume of the new series.

The policy of the publishers to print the old records of the Colony of Virginia will be adhered to, but the value of the publication will be enhanced by the additional Heraldic data, which will cover the armigerous families of the United States and Canada.

Certificates and confirmations of arms under Seal of the College are granted to all those who can prove descent from an armigerous ancestor, upon payment of the fees for certification.

There are no fees to be paid, unless the applicant is granted a certificate.

Residents of the United States may make application through the Deputy-Commissioner, William Armstrong Crozier, F.R.S., F.G.S.A., Hasbrouck Heights, New Jersey.

College of Arms of Canada

Founded by Edict of King Louis XIV., in 1664. Confirmed by Royal Commission of the Appeal of Malta 1877.

OFFICERS.

The Baron de Longueuil, Chancellor of the Aryan and Seigneuria. Orders.

The Viscount de Fronsac, Herald-Marshal, Huntingdon, P. Q., Canada, Hon. Thomas Scott Forsyth, Registrar-General, 19 Hanover Street. Montreal, Canada.

COMMISSIONERS.

Henry Black Stuart, Esq., C. E., Sexton Villa, Westmount, Montreal, Canada.
Rev. J. B. Pyke, M. A., 19 Hanover Street. Montreal, Canada.

SOLICITOR-GENERAL IN THE UNITED STATES.

Sir John Calder Gordon, 17 Milk Street, Boston, Mass.

DEPUTY COMMISSIONER IN THE UNITED STATES.

William Armstrong Crozier, Esq., F. R. S., F. G. S. A., Hasbrouck Heights, N. J.

YELLOW ROSE PERSUYVANT.

J. G. B. Bulloch, Esq., M. D., 2122 P. Street, N. W. Washington, D. C.

REPRESENTATIVE IN GREAT BRITAIN.

The Marquis de Ruvigny, 14 Hanover Chambers, Buckingham St., Strand, W. C., London.

REPRESENTATIVE IN FRANCE.

M. Louis Denys de Bonaventure, Chateau d'Aytre, Charente Inferieure.

OFFICIAL PUBLICATION.

The Virginia County Records and Heraldic Quarterly Register of the United States and Canada.

CONTENTS

Virginia County Records

AND HERALDIC QUARTERLY REGISTER

VOL. IX (OLD SERIES)
VOL. I (NEW SERIES) **1911** **Part 4**

INDEX TO LAND GRANTS

KING GEORGE LAND GRANTS.

BOOK A.

Book B.

Book C.

BOOK D.

19	Thomas Turner	1731	33
58	Saml. Skinker	1731	90
77	Dr. Thos. Turner	1731	35
78	Simon Sallard	1731	710
79	Rawleigh Chinn	1731	504
80	Alex. Beach	1731	185
99	Jeremiah Murdock	1732	374

BOOK E.

8	Simon Sallard	1737	710
9	Jeremiah Murdock	1737	374
11	John Piper	1737	37
58	Catesby Cocke	1739	200
87	Alex. Beach	1739	185
88	Rowland Thornton	1739	17
89	Rawleigh Chinn	1739	504
91	Wm. Duff	1739	1539
114	Lewis Elroy	1739	160
142	Charles Carter	1739	1997
149	Samuel Moon	1740	60
176	Richard Bryant	1740	49
238	Hon. John Tayloe	1740	50

BOOK F.

79	Capt. Augustine Washington	1742	289
203	Major Lawrence Washington	1744	170
324	Le Roy Griffin	1749	1880
291	Capt. Joseph Strother	1748	94

BOOK I.

175	William Allason	1770	676

BOOK T.

408	James Brown and Cath., his wife	1789	105

BOOK V.

202	Woffendall Kendall	1791	33
204	Same	1791	45
318	Same	1791	82

Book X.

Book No. 1.

HALIFAX LAND GRANTS

(Continued).

Book No. 34.

Book No. 35.

174	John Talbot	1763	82
175	Wm. Shelton	1763	80
175	Joseph East	1763	400
176	John Callaway	1763	314
177	James Breadlow	1763	387
177	John Bostick	1763	404
179	Abraham Abney	1763	400
180	Same	1763	343
201	Samuel Bynum	1763	300
215	Wm. Goare	1763	400
224	Geo. Watkins	1763	390
225	Francis Bucknall	1763	300
229	Robert Innis, clerk	1763	244
230	George Lumkin	1763	370
234	Jeremiah Morrow	1763	260
238	Henry Rice	1763	200
242	Richard Welton	1763	200
244	Thos. Wilson	1763	385
245	Thos. Williamson	1763	400
246	Peter Wilson	1763	150
264	David Powell	1763	400
267	Benj. Dickson	1763	1061
271	Jas. Stewart	1763	254
276	Wm. Callaway	1763	450
280	John Goad	1763	400
291	Wm. Rickel	1763	354
294	Peter Wilson	1763	104
301	Wm. East and Wm. East, Jr.	1763	780
308	Fredk. Fulkerson	1763	40
312	Lewis Jenkins	1763	387
313	Henry McDaniel	1763	400
314	Henry Print	1763	354
322	Matt. Marrable	1763	325
323	Same	1763	300
324	George Walton	1763	10,000
345	John Robinson, Esq	1763	7384
347	Richard Witton	1763	200

348	And. Shepherd	1763	11,267
356	Richard Brown	1763	2900
384	Joseph Cameron	1763	400
385	Samuel Gordon	1763	440
386	Same	1763	400
386	Same	1763	380
387	John Coleman	1763	230
388	James Cox	1763	400
389	Wm. Powell	1763	234
390	Joseph Madcalf	1763	346
391	Aaron Williams	1763	400
392	Same	1763	404
447	Alex. Moore	1763	400
452	Wm. Dendy	1763	350
452	Rich'd Brown	1763	704
453	Wm. Roysdon	1763	300
455	Wm. Bean	1763	800
479	Saml. Jones	1764	276
481	Stephen Cocke	1764	336
505	Wm. Jones	1764	3000
507	David Logan, Jr.	1764	217
509	Wm. Mead	1764	185
512	John Moutray	1764	400
522	Thos. Spraggons	1764	325
523	James Stewart	1764	485
526	John Tribble	1764	400
529	John Ward	1764	210
530	Robert Wooding	1764	154
531	John Wynfrey	1764	597
532	Wm. Wickett	1764	382
532	John Wilcox	1764	403
533	Robt. Wooding	1764	247
535	Jno. Wilcox	1764	400
537	George Abney	1764	400
550	Archibald Grymes	1764	400

Book No. 36.

557	Wm. Mead	1764	183
578	Thos. Clarke, Jr.	1764	400
579	John Clarke	1764	400
583	Clement Reade, Jr.	1764	8000
586	John Lynch	1764	287
589	Crespin Shelton	1764	1515
595	Anthony Irby	1764	774
596	Richard Adams	1764	5470
601	Owen Brady	1764	400
604	Joseph Byrd	1764	250
606	John Butler	1764	435
607	Same	1764	400
608	James Cooley	1764	295
609	Joseph Collins	1764	400
610	Edward Cahall	1764	217
613	Elisha Eastis	1764	260
619	Thomas Grisam	1764	400
622	James and Charles Hunt	1764	820
623	John Hamilton	1764	400
628	Wm. Irvine	1764	100
635	Henry Lansford	1764	383
635	George Lumkin	1764	394
639	Wm. McDaniel	1764	299
640	Wm. Mead	1764	470
648	Nicholas Perkins	1764	90
651	Peter Perkins	1764	820
665	John Watson	1764	220
667	Zachariah Waller	1764	400
674	John Adams	1764	314
684	Wm. Echols	1764	1041
689	John Legrand	1764	975
703	James Owen	1764	390
707	Joseph Terry	1764	400
709	Wm. Williams	1764	266
715	Sam'l Harris	1765	400
717	Peter Legrand	1765	804

722	Peter Royster	1765	356
724	Chas. Clay	1765	400
728	Jno. Harris and Valentine Gibson	1765	404
735	Thos. Daugherty	1765	400
739	Theophilus Field	1765	3800
740	Jeremiah Hatcher	1765	1616
743	Anthony Street and Wm. Hawkins, Jr.	1765	250
743	Sherwood Walton	1765	1200
746	John Donaldson	1765	281
748	George Green	1765	104
753	Wm. Payne	1765	435
755	Thomas Dendy	1765	908
755	Richard Keesee	1765	320
765	Richard Wilton	1765	5316
770	Robert Wooding	1765	800
782	Archibald Gordon	1765	400
788	Joseph Terry	1765	1580
792	Charles Little	1765	400
794	John Lankford	1765	360
798	Robt. Wooding	1765	160
804	Jacob Chancey	1765	380
805	Thos. Waters	1765	400
805	Jas. Shoekley	1765	400
806	Seth Pettypool	1765	383
809	Jas. Hollins	1765	400
820	John Sutton	1765	135
821	Nathaniel Terry	1765	170
823	Same	1765	400
823	John Wall	1765	400
830	Peter Fountain	1765	2805
833	Jas. Norrell	1765	262
836	Reuben Paine	1765	150
854	Tully Choice	1765	400
859	Peter Wilson	1765	150
861	Sam'l Preuit	1765	335
861	Ambrose Haley	1765	275
865	Thos. Fambrough	1765	400

868	Robt. Wooding	1765	137
868	Jas. Spradlen	1765	302
874	Wm. Sizemore	1765	200
881	Robert Wooding	1765	400
884	Thomas Mann Randolph, John Harmer and Walter King	1765	4580
885	John More	1765	390
887	Joseph Akin	1765	370
888	John Armstrong	1765	65
894	Peter Fountain	1765	400
896	Patrick Shields	1765	51
901	David Wilson	1765	400
905	Thos. M. Randolph, John Harmer and Walter King	1765	5520
908	Same	1765	11,565
910	Champness Terry	1765	20,000
916	Thomas Sayers	1765	380
925	Stephen Herd	1765	229
933	John Cox	1765	400
935	Charles Clay	1766	9600
940	Lewis Jenkins	1766	350
944	Matthew Marrable	1766	350
958	Wm. McDaniel	1766	3620
967	Robt. Walters	1766	120
972	David Evans	1766	160
972	Sam'l Gordon	1766	330
973	Same	1766	3450
979	Geo. Carter	1766	185
983	Alman Gwin	1766	380
986	Thos. Davenport	1766	360
993	Wm. Rice	1766	90
999	Henry Burnett	1766	250
1000	Peter Wilson	1766	125
1000	David Chadwell	1766	237
1002	Swinfield Hill	1766	150
1003	Thos. Jones	1766	140
1004	Nicholas Lankford	1766	150

1006	David Witt and Palatiah Shelton	1766	400
1006	Jonathan Jones	1766	386
1007	John Dyer	1766	400
1008	Lazers Dodson	1766	400
1008	Peter Cornwall	1766	300
1011	John Bynum	1766	400
1013	Saml. Harris	1766	160
1014	Wm. Rice	1766	135
1018	Wm. McDaniel	1766	850
1019	Wm. Haynes	1766	243
1020	Wm. Stamps	1766	365
1020	Sam'l Preuit	1766	350
1026	Thos. Spraggins	1767	400
1026	Wm. Spraggin	1767	182
1030	Robt. Peak	1767	277
1033	John Loving	1767	400
1062	Joseph Collins	1767	400
1063	Thos. Conner	1767	348
1065	Wm. Tweedwell	1767	400
1080	John Fitzgerald	1767	400

LYON FAMILY.

Contributed by Dr. J. L. Miller.

Bible records of Col. James Lyon, Sr., of Henry County, Va., now in possession of Mrs. Helen Deas of New York City, a daughter of Hon. Francis Strother Lyon of Alabama, shows the following:

"Col. James Lyon, born in March, 1736, departed this life the 29th Dec., 1817, in the 81st year of his age." (In Stokes County, N. C.)

"Christiana Lyon (1st), wife of Col. James Lyon, died Feb. 23, 1784."

"Maj. Stephen Lyon, oldest son of James and Christiana Lyon, departed this life on the 20th of May, 1820, in Granger County, Tenn."

"Humberson Lyon, departed this life the 20 July, 1793."

"Sarah Lyon, second wife of Col. J. S. Lyon, departed this life 6th August, 1815, in Stokes County, N. C."

"James Lyon, born in Henry County, Virginia, Dec. 25, 1778, died in Stokes County, N. C., August 30, 1849. Son of Col. James Lyon." James Lyon, Jr., married in April, 1797, Behethland Gaines and had sons James Gaines Lyon and Francis Strother Lyon, both of Alabama.

Feb. 28, 1795, James Lyon, Sr., purchased a tract of land in Patrick County, Va.; and Dec. 25, 1797, James Lyon, Sr., James Lyon, Jr., and Miller Easley conveyed the same to Gabriel Penn. No other Lyon appears in the Patrick records until in 1863 the inventory and sale bill of the estate of a James Lyon was recorded.

The Preston Register shows that a Stephen Lyon was killed by the Indians in 1754 on the Holston River, in Washington County. He may have been a brother of James Lyon of Henry County, and may have been the father of the Kentucky Lyon emigrants.

The Journal of Capt. Robert Wade shows that a James Lyon was a member of his company of men who made an expedition on New River against the Indians on Saturday, August 12, 1758. Perhaps this was James of Henry County, who at that time might have been a resident of Washington.

The old Fincastle surveys show that a Humberson Lyon had a survey on May 26, 1774, for 343 acres of land on the North Fork of Holston River, in what later was Washington County. The Military rosters of this county for 1777-1782 give the names of Lt. Humberson Lyon, Capt. Humberson Lyon (probably the same man), and Lt. William Lyon. Summer's Hist. of Southwest Va. gives in a list of those killed at the Battle of King's Mt. the name of Lt. Humberson Lyon.

THE KENTUCKY LYON FAMILY.

Joseph Lyon, was settled on Lyon's Run, Mercer County, Ky., in Dec., 1775, when he with 83 other inhabitants of "that part of North America now dominated Transylvania" signed and sent to the Virginia legislature an energetic protest against the unreasonable demands of Col. Richard Henderson and his company, and praying to be taken under the protection of the government of Virginia.

In 1785 he contributed to the erection of "New Providence" Presbyterian church in Mercer County, also to be used for school purposes.

Sept. 26, 1803, Joseph Lyon and wife Jane conveyed to Ezekial Lyon, 80 acres "on Lyon's Run," Mercer Co., Ky. When this land came into his possession can not be learned. The 80 acres was but a part of the tract. July 24, 1803, Joseph Lyon purchased 250 acres on McAfee's Run, Mercer County; and July 22, 1810, a tract of 150 acres on Lyon's Run.

Sept. 18, 1833, John Lyon gave to brother Robert Lyon a quit-claim deed to their father Joseph Lyon's estate.

Oct. 4, 1842, Joseph Lyon's heirs, viz.: Nancy Kennedy, Stephen, George, John, and Robert Lyon, by Commissioner made partition deeds to John and Robert. Stephen Lyon (my great grandfather) married in 1819 Anne Curran, daughter of James and Sarah McAfee Curran, and granddaughter of Robert McAfee, the younger of the McAfee brothers, famous as early explorers and settlers in Mercer County, Ky. She was a niece of Gen. Robt. Breckenridge McAfee, who was Lt-Gov. of Kentucky 1824-'28, a member of the two branches of the Ky. Legislature for twenty years, U. S. Minister to the U. S. of Colombia 1833-'37, etc.

Ezekial Lyon, supposed to have been a brother of Joseph Lyon, was also settled in Mercer County for several years prior to 1800, though the deed for his first tract of land in this county is not of record in the county except when he conveyed it away later. Dec. 26, 1797. is the date of first deed Ezekial Lyon recorded in Mercer. However, his son David Lyon had a deed for 100 acres on Salt River, Mercer Co., Va., from Geo. & Susannah McAfee on Apr. 28, 1789. And Ezekial's son John Lyon had a deed for 130 acres in Mercer Co., Ky., from Heirs of Job Hale on May 26, 1795.

Ezekial Lyon's will prob. in July, 1839, left good estate to wife, Martha and sons and daughters, Stephen, John, David,

William, Polly Cochran, Sally Renear, Elizabeth Cochran, and Susan Lyon, and the children of a deceased daughter who had married Jos. McGee.

The Mercer records contain much other data of the later descendants of Joseph and Ezekial Lyon, among whom the names of James and Stephen appear.

HILL OF MIDDLESEX.

In the "Baltimore Sun" of March 1, 1908, an erroneous pedigree of the early history of the Hill family was published. The following data has been compiled from the existing records of the county:

There were two families of the same name residing in Middlesex, viz.: Thomas Hill and his wife Ann, of whom we are about to speak, and a William Hill, who also had a wife Ann. What degree of relationship existed, if any, between these two men the records do not show.

The "Sun" pedigree states, without the least attempt at authority, that "Thomas Hill married Ann Russell, who was descended from Sir William Russell, or John Russell, who came to Virginia about 1620." Such an assertion is ridiculous. There was no Sir William or Sir John Russell in Virginia at that date, or, in fact, at any other date. It is quite possible that Thomas Hill did marry an Ann Russell, as there was a family living in Middlesex of that name, and Thomas Hill's grandson was named Russell Hill. The "Sun" writer also states that Thomas Hill's father was William Hill. There was a William Hill who was buried in the churchyard of Christ Church 12 Feb., 1669, but there is no evidence that he was the father of Thomas. According to the parish register and the will and deed books, Thomas and Ann Hill had the following issue:

1. Mary, born 14 Feb., 1678.
2. Rebecca, born 30 August, 1682.
3. William, baptized 20 July, 1684.

4. Rebecca (2nd of the name), born 28 Nov., 1686; m. 31
   Dec., 1704, to John Hughes.
5. Isabella, born 1 May, 1698; m. 20 May, 1729, to John
   Jones.
6. Richard, born ———.

Several of the early record books of Middlesex have been
lost, and the will of Thomas Hill is missing. From the Court
Order book we find that "Mr. Thomas Hill was a member of
the county militia 23rd November, 1687." Richard Hill, a son
of Thomas, left a will dated 18 Jan., 1731, probated 2 May,
1732. He left no living issue, and devises most of his estate
to his brother William and the latter's children.

William Hill, son of Thomas and Ann Hill, married 7
Sept., 1710, Frances Needles. According to the "Sun," she
was a daughter of John Needles and his wife Elizabeth Mann.
This is a mistake. There is no record of the above named having a daughter Frances; it was Mr. William Needles and his
wife Dorothy who had a daughter named Frances, born 19
March, 1690. (Par. Reg.) Issue of William Hill and his
wife Frances:

1. Thomas, born 20 May, 1711; died 3 August, 1720.
2. William, born 7 Nov., 1712. His estate was adm. by his
   brother Russell Hill, 2 Jan., 1759.
3. Richard, born 15 Jan., 1714; died 23 Jan., 1714.
4. Russell, born 23 Feb., 1717.
5. Judith, born 2 June, 1719; married 22 Jan., 1738, to William Booton.
6. Thomas, born 17 June, 1722.
7 Needles, born 12 August, 1725.
8. Frances, born 26 Jan., 1727; died 30 May, 1746.
9. Anne, born 25 July, 1730.

Russell Hill, 4th son of William and Frances Hill, married 11 April, 1738, Anne, a daughter of Stokeley and Ann
Towles of Middlesex, born 23 April, 1719. They moved to
what is now Culpeper and had issue:

1. Frances, born 25 Feb., 1738; died 12 March, 1738.
2. William, born ———; married Mary Jane Wood.

3. Henry, born 1743.

4. Frances, 2nd of the name, born ———.

Henry Hill, 2nd son of Russell and Anne Hill, died 12 Sept., 1815. He married Ann Powell, born 10 March, 1752, a daughter of Captain Ambrose Powell, born 18 Sept., 1713, died 18 Sept., 1788; married 10 March, 1752, to Mary Bledsoe, who died 10 Jan., 1802, a daughter of Captain William Bledsoe and Mary, his wife. Henry Hill served as Captain in the Revolutionary War from 1777 under Col. James Barbour (War Dept., File S, 7771). According to the family records, he was promoted to the rank of Colonel, and served under "Light Horse" Harry Lee. Henry Hill and his wife Ann had issue:

1. Colonel Robert Hill, born 7 Oct., 1772; died 14 Aug., 1824; married Judith Chapman and left issue.

2. Frances, born 5 August, 1775; died 1853; married Henry Field and left issue.

3. William, born 11 May, 1779; died 10 July, 1803.

4. Henry, born 5 October, 1782; died — Feb., 1846: married Mattie Payne.

5. Captain Ambrose Powell Hill, born 13 March, 1785: died 26 Feb., 1858; married 10 Feb. (1st wife) Fannie Twyman, born 27 April, 1789; died 18 Sept., 1820; daughter of William Twyman, born in Culpeper in 1754, and was Orderly Sergeant in the Revolution from 1777 to 1781, being at the seige and surrender of Yorktown. Captain Ambrose Hill was Captain of the Culpeper Minute Men during the War of 1812; member of the State Legislature and Senate for 20 years. He left issue.

6   Ann, born 5 Oct., 1786; died 30 Sept., 1842; married Rev. Thornton Str.ngfellow.

7. Thomas, born 3 Oct., 1789; died 5 Jan., 1857; married Frances R. Baptist, and was the father of the celebrated Confederate General Ambrose P. Hill, born 1825; killed at Petersburg, 2 April, 1865.

Needles Hill, born 12 August, 1725, son of William and Frances Hill; married 1st Jane Morgan, by her he had a son Humphrey, born in 1755. It is evident he married 2nd Letitia Morgan, Marriage Bond, 4 Oct., 1758, who may have been a sister of Jane. The will of William Morgan of Midd., probated 3 April, 1764, mentions his daughter Letitia Hill and his son-in-law Needles Hill, who was one of the exors. Needles Hill had three known children, the first at least by Jane:

1. Humphrey, born 7 April, 1755.
2. Frances.
3. Mary.

NORTHAMPTON COUNTY MARRIAGE BONDS.

(Continued from Vol. VII.)

Dec. 13, 1791. Michael Dunton, Jr., and Peggy Griffin.
June 23, 1791. Thos. Dixon and Betty, dau. of Richard Smith, Sr.
Jan. 25, 1791. John Downing and Edy Nottingham.
July 18, 1791. John Dixon and Nelly, dau. of Abraham Costin.
June 7, 1791. Thos. Douty and Sarah, dau. of William Belote, decd.
Jan. 20, 1791. Teackle Dennis and Patty Hall.
Sept. 29, 1791. Wm. Dennis and Susanna, dau. of John Whitehead, decd.
Nov. 20, 1792. Carney Dunton and Margaret Robins.
Apr. 10, 1792. Severn Dunton and Mary Bryan, widow of Levin Bryan.
July 3, 1792. Michael Dunton and Sarah Bell, widow of Thomas Bell.
Mar. 7, 1793. Thomas Dixon and Anne Nottingham.
Jan. 23, 1793. Nathan Drighouse and Elizabeth Bingham.
July 16, 1794. Thomas Dunton and Sukey Bell.
Aug. 28, 1794. Littleton Dalby and Bridget Fisher.
June 8, 1795. Thomas Dalby and Priscilla Rogers.

Nov. 24. 1795. William Dorman and Peggy Dunton.

Nov. 4, 1795. Moses Driskell and Margaret Joynes.

Nov. 22, 1796. Dr. Thomas Drysdale and Mary Anne dau. of Isaac Smith.

Aug. 13, 1796. Rickards Dunton, Jr., and Rosanna Clegg.

Aug. 2, 1797. Thomas Dowty and Susanna Turner.

June 3, 1797. Benjamin Dunton and Sarah Garrison.

Mar. 2, 1798. George Drighouse and Peggy Lang.

May 25, 1798. Isaac Dalby and Catherine Dalby.

June 4, 1798. William Dillon and Nancy Fisher.

July 6, 1798. Babel Dowty and Betsy Hickman.

Oct. 8, 1798. John Downell and Anne Teackle Smith, dau. of Isaac Smith.

Dec. 27, 1797. William Downs and Elizabeth Warren.

Mar. 26, 1800. Thomas Dunton and Polly Hanby.

Jan. 8, 1800. William Dennis and Ann Caple.

Dec. 22, 1800. John Dunton and Sukey Mills.

May 23, 1801. Edward Davidson and Jenny McMeth.

June 3, 1715. George Esdall and Esther, dau. of George Green.

Apr. 21, 1727. John Ellegood and Ellinor Jacob.

Mar. 12, 1732. Nicholas Eyre and Ann Mifflin.

Mar. 21, 1734. Nicholas Eyre and Isabel Harmanson.

Jan. 15, 1734. Littleton Eyre and Bridgett Harmanson.

Nov. 5, 1735. Peter Norley Ellegood and Margaret Forse, widow.

May 12, 1748. John Ellegood and Susanna Wilkins, widow.

May 17, 1755. Levin Evans and Ann Mary Pitts.

Mar. 19, 1752. John Ellegood and Esther Wilkins.

June 7, 1763. Gustavus Ewing and Elizabeth James, widow.

Mar. 15, 1764. John Ellegood and Nancy, dau. of Abel Powell, decd.

Aug. 26, 1765. Wm. Evans and Ada, dau. of Jonathan Widgeon, decd.

Sept. 14, 1768. William Ellegood of Worcester Co., Md., and Sarah Powell, dau. of Abel Powell, decd.

Feb.   7, 1774.   John Evans and Peggy, dau. of William Simkins.
July 16, 1774.   William Elliott and Rose, dau. of John Johnson, decd.
Mar. 17, 1777.   Ellegood Eyre and Esther, dau. of James Saunders.
Sept. 12, 1777.   Arthur Evans and Ada Kemp, widow.
Dec. 31, 1782.   Richard Evans and Elizabeth Goffigon, dau. of Sarah Biggs.
Aug. 10, 1784.   Thomas Elliott and Keziah Turner.
Nov. 28, 1785.   John Ewing and Jane Holbrook.
——— —, 1786.   Edward Esdell and Elizabeth, widow of Charles Floyd.
Jan. 28, 1788.   Jonathan Ellegood and Esther, widow of William Floyd.
May   21, 1790.   William Evans and Rebecca, widow of William Wood.
Aug. 30, 1792.   John Elliott and Mary Abdell, widow.
June 21, 1796.   Arthur Evans and Nelly Dove (or Deve).
Feb.   3, 1798.   Thomas Edmons and Peggy Hanby.
Oct. 22, 1800.   Thomas Edmunds and Rosey Dennis.
Jan. 10, 1799.   Nathaniel Esdall and Betty Luke.
Nov. 17, 1800.   John Evans and Sauteky Moore.
Feb. 24, 1800.   John Eyre and Anne, dau. of Abel Upshur.
Aug.   1, 1801.   Thomas Elliott and Sally Widgeon.
Dec. 18, 1801.   John Elliott and Polly Nolm.
May   13, 1709.   Harmon Firkettle and Frances Cowdry.
July 15, 1752.   Nehemiah Fitchett and Elizabeth Flood.
Dec. 24, 1746.   William Finney and Joanna Scott, widow.
July 11, 1752.   John Flood and Frances Warren, widow.
Aug.   1, 1754.   Thomas Fisher and Sarah Turner, widow.
Mar. 24, 1763.   Jacob Freshwater and Mary, dau. of John Nelson, decd.
Dec.   8, 1762.   Charles Floyd and Sarah, dau. of Jacob Williams, decd.
June 24, 1761.   John Lewis Fulwell and Margaret, dau. of Jacob Costin.

July 22, 1762.   Nehemiah Fitchett and Rachael Stringer, widow.
Apr. 16, 1765.   Esme Fisher and Margaret Roberts, widow.
Feb. 14, 1765.   John Floyd and Margaret, dau. of Mathew Floyd, Jr., decd.
Jan. 11, 1769.   Colin Fraser and Elinor Waterfield.
Apr. 14, 1772.   Wm. Floyd and Esther, dau, of John Kendall, decd.
May 15, 1770.   Thomas Fisher and Margaret, dau. of Michael Christian.
Aug. 21, 1773.   John Floyd and Mary, dau. of John Brickhouse.
July 12, 1774.   Serafino Formicola and Matilda Newman, widow.
Sept. 6, 1775.   Caleb Fisher and Elizabeth, dau. of Zerubabel Downing.
Mar. 6, 1775.   William Fourshee and Isabel Harmanson.
Sept. 25, 1776.   William Fisher and Rose, dau. of Wm. Christian, decd.
Mar. 3, 1778.   Charles Floyd and Elizabeth, dau. of John Tamkard.
Nov. 25, 1782.   Robert Fitchett and Sally Warren.
Nov. 12, 1782.   Joshua Fitchett and Sukey Dixon.
Nov. 27, 1782.   Joseph Frost and Eleanor Walker, dau. of John Walker.
Jan. 15, 1783.   Jonathan Fitchett and Elizabeth Nottingham.
Nov. 11, 1786.   William Freshwater and Nancy Miles.
Nov. 30, 1787.   Jonathan Fitchett and Nancy, dau. of Nathl. Tyson.
Apr. 20, 1787.   Samuel Flood and Sarah Chance.
Sept. 20, 1787.   Jacob Fatherly and Esther Bell.
Dec. 21, 1789.   Henry Fitchett and Ann Heutage.
Feb. 12, 1789.   William Fisher and Sally, dau. of Powell Johnson, decd.
Oct. 13, 1789.   George Fisher and Susanna Joynes.
Mar. 12, 1790.   Stephen Fletcher and Susan Churn.
Dec. 22, 1790.   Mathew Floyd and Sarah Robins, widow.

Dec. 27, 1790. Robert Fitchett and Frances Wilkins Widgeon.

Dec. 13, 1791. James Fisher and Mary, dau. of William White, decd.

Dec. 30, 1791. William Francis and Polly Jacob.

Mar. 1, 1791. John Frost and Betty Knight.

Dec. 28, 1792. John Francis and Ibby Sheppard, widow.

Oct. 2, 1793. Caleb Fisher and Elizabeth West.

July 31, 1794. Mathew Floyd and Nancy Wilson.

Aug. 25, 1795. John Fitchew (Fitzhugh ?) and Molly Luke.

Sept. 13, 1795. Dr. Victor Augustus Fulwell and Elizabeth Simkins.

Jan. 13, 1796. James Fletcher and Nanny Churn.

Jan. 13, 1796. William Fletcher and Sarah Churn.

Dec. 26, 1796. Thomas Francis and Tabby Press.

(Continued.)

AMELIA COUNTY MARRIAGE BONDS.

(Continued from Vol. IV.)

Feb. 20, 1746. Peter Jones and Sarah Farmer.

June 15, 1744. William Osborne and Elizabeth Tanner.

——— —, 1745. William Childers and Keturah Hawkins.

Oct. 2, 1749. George Booker and Sarah Cobbs. Sec. Richard Booker.

Dec. 2, 1745. John Clement and Frances Booker. Sec. Edwd. Booker, Jr.

July 16, 1739. Nicholas Darwin and Eliz. Jones. Sec. John Jones.

June 28, 1746. William Giles and Mary M. Ellis. Sec. John Ellis.

Oct. 25, 1746. Henry Warde and Prudence Jones.

June 17, 17—. Benj. Williamson and Mary Green.

Jan. 20, 1748. Joseph Ward and Martha Burton. Sec. John Burton.

Sept. 22, 1739. William Watson and Mary Jones.

Feb. 21, 1739.   Edward Booker and Ann Cobbs.
Jan. 26, 1749.   Richard Burke and Milly Hawkins.   Sec.
                 Benj. Hawkins.
May 17, 1746.   Edmund Booker and Edith Cobbs.
Nov. 17, 1747.   Benjamin Cheatham and Grace Williams.
Feb. —, 1749.   Mathew Branch and ————.
Sept. 4, 1745.   Gideon Marr and Sarah Miller.
June 3, 1745.   Thomas Lorton and Elizabeth Moss, widow.
—— —, 1745-6.   John Booker and Phoebe Worsham.
July 9, 1742.   Francis Anderson and Edith Weldon.
Sept. 18, 1741. Thomas Spencer and Elizabeth ————.
July 25, 1754.   Thomas Spain (or Spann) and Eliz. Mayo.
                 Sec. Jno. Mayo.
Sept. 27, 1735. Thos. Tabb and Rebecca Booker.   Sec. Rich-
                 ard Booker.
May 2, 1750.   Roger Thomson and Ann Ferguson.
July 13, 1750.   William Williamson and Martha Green.
Jan. 15, 1752.   Joel Watkins and Rhoda Gresham.
Nov. 2, 1752.   Sampson Meredith and Sarah Stearnson.
Mar. 30, 1752.   Fredk. Spain and Mary Roberts.
Feb. 11, 1755.   Robert Munford and Ann Brodnax.
—— —, 1753.   John Mayes and ———— Spain.
Apr. 1, 1755.   William Booker and Mary Flournoy.   Sec.
                 Edwd. Booker, Jr.
Oct. 8, 1751.   William Easton and Catherine Neal.
Nov. 9, 1754.   Richard Ellis and Mary Cocke.
May 15, 1751.   William Daniel and Agnes Markham.   Sec.
                 Wm. Daniel.
Apr. 17, 1755.   Richd. Claiborne and Mary Hamlin.   Sec.
                 Thomas Claiborne.
Nov. 27, 1754.   Anthony Chishom and Mary Watkins.
Oct. 2, 1752.   David Holt and Betty Hall.
Nov. 24, 1752.   Leland Ward and ———— Jones, dau. of Rich-
                 ard Jones.
June 16, 1750.   Robert Jones and Sarah Scott.
Nov. 19, 1750.   James Roberts and Susannah Ellis.   Sec.
                 Richard Ellis.

Dec. 31, 1750.   John Royall and Elizabeth Worsham.
Apr. 6, 1752.   William Walthall and Anna Elam.
May 24, 1755.   Filmer Wills and Eliz. Rebecca Green. Sec. Abra. Green.
Nov. 24, 1752.   Rowland Ward and Rebecca Jones. Sec. Richard Jones.
Jan. 17, 1753.   Joseph Boswell and Eliz. Elliott. Sec. Geo. Elliott.
Feb. 4, 1755.   John Banister and Elizabeth Munford.
Sept. 11, 1750.   John Coms and Frances Elam.
Mar. 4, 1761.   Richard Anderson and Jane Foster. Sec. Thos. Anderson.
Nov. 15, 1784.   Reynard Anderson and Mary Ford.
Apr. 9, 1789.   Matthew Anderson and Polly, dau. of George Bagley.
May 1, 1790.   Francis Anderson and Sally Anderson Blackburn.
Mar. —, 1800.   Churchill Anderson and Polly Goode.

(Continued.)

PITTSYLVANIA MARRIAGE BONDS.

Feb. 2, 1770.   Thomas Dudley and Susanna Burton.
Mar. 24, 1770.   Lewis Salmon and Margaret, dau. of Thomas Shannon.
Aug. 23, 1770.   Edmund King and Mary Thomas.
Mar. 3, 1770.   Charles Williams and Ann Wilson.
Feb. 10, 1767.   Richard White and Margaret Donald.
Sept. 27, 1767.   Samuel Dalton, Jr., and Charlotte Gallitice.
Nov. 25, 1768.   Ambrose Bramlett and Jean Woodson, dau. of John and Charity Burch.
Nov. 25, 1768.   James Mitchell and Agatha, dau. of Robert Dalton.
Feb. 24, 1769.   William Owen and Edey, dau. of John Pigg.
Mar. 24, 1769.   Jonathan Hanby and Sarah Dalton.
Aug. 25, 1769.   Adonijah Harbour and Ann, dau. of Samuel Dalton.

Aug. 25, 1769.   Archelaus Hughes and Mary, dau. of Samuel Dalton.

Dec. 16, 1769.   Munford Smith and Catherine Armstrong.

Dec. 25. 1769.   Beverley Shelton and Anne Coleman.

Feb. 13, 1771.   David Hanby and Jenny, dau. of Samuel Dalton.

Mar. 28, 1771.   Jesse Robinson and Betsey, dau. of John Pigg.

Dec. 17, 1771.   Spilsbee Coleman and Judith, dau. of Robert Burton.

Aug. 30, 1773.   William Ryburn and Mary Terry. Sec. Ben. Terry.

Feb. 7, 1774.   William Todd and Jean, dau. of Crispin Shelton.

Apr. 19, 1774.   William Lovell and Mary Dudley.

Sept. —, 1774.   Armistead Shelton and Susanna, dau. of Daniel Shelton.

Apr. —, 1775.   Edmund Taylor and Milicent, dau. of Daniel Shelton.

Dec. 14, 1776.   Samuel Calland and Elizabeth Smith, with consent of brother Ralph Smith.

Apr. 3, 1777.   Edward Covington and Fanny Prewitt.

June 26, 1777.   Samuel Johnston and Elizabeth, dau. of Joseph Ballinger.

Aug. 28, 1777.   John Thurston and Susannah, dau. of W. Pace.

Sept. 27, 1777.   John Morton and Lucy, dau. of James Blackley.

Nov. 15, 1777.   John May and Susannah Porter. Sec. Joseph Porter.

Nov. 26, 1777.   Joseph Austin and Wealthy Prewitt.

Feb. 6, 1778.   Caleb Hundley and Sarah, dau. of Joseph Walker.

Mar. 26, 1778.   John Wier and Sally, dau. of Charles Burton.

May 6, 1778.   Joseph Morton and Clarey Harrison.

July 25, 1778.   John Whitwell and Catherine Aaron.

Oct. 7, 1778.   Daniel White and Molly Wade. Sec. John White.

Oct. 13, 1778.   Lemuel Smith and Bethania, dau. of Peter Perkins.

Oct. 22, 1778.   Levi Prewitt and Elizabeth, dau. of John Taliaferro.

Nov. 20, 1778.   William Letcher and Elizabeth Perkins.

Aug. 17, 1779.   John Donelson and Mary Purnell, consent of mother Mary Purnell.

Sept. 17, 1779.   Ezekiel Vincent and Eliz. Cooley. Sec. Jacob Cooley.

May 19, 1779.   David Reace and Nancy Cooley. Sec. Jacob Cooley.

Sept. 21, 1779.   Joshua Dodson and Ann, dau. of Charles Chilton.

Feb. 25, 1779.   William Hardaway and Polly White. Sec. Jere White.

Feb. 6, 1778.   Caleb Hundley and Sarah, dau. of Joseph Walker.

Mar. 11, 1779.   Charles Keith and Archer Clarke.

Mar. 16, 1779.   William Asten and Margaret Wilson.

Apr. 26, 1779.   Sarting Willis and Sarah, dau. of Wm. Payne.

June 19, 1779.   Wm. Vincent and Glassey, dau. of Jacob Cooley.

July 20. 1779.   William Wilkinson and Sally Dix. Sec. John Dix.

July 21, 1779.   Caleb Brewer and Polly Hundley.

Oct. 19, 1779.   Clement McDaniel and Eliz. Coleman. Sec. Stephen Coleman.

Nov. 21, 1779.   David Gamble and Margaret Razon. Sec. Paul Razon.

Dec. 21, 1779.   Samuel Parsons and Beckey Farthing.

Mar. 2, 1780.   Enoch Ward Ellington and Sarah, dau. of Tucker and Judith Woodson.

WAR DEPARTMENT RECORDS.

Christopher Freeman, served as soldier in the Virginia Infantry, Revolutionary War. His name appears on a list of soldiers of the Virginia Line Continental establishment, which shows that a certificate for 29 pounds 12 shillings, the balance of his full pay, was on December 1, 1785, received by a Mr. Wilkins. (Adjutant General's Office. 1763928 A.)

William Twyman of Culpeper, served as Orderly Sergeant in the Revolutionary War. Enlisted August or September, 1777, for 2 months and served under Captain Henry Hill, James Barbour Pendleton, Colonel. Re-enlisted Jan., 1781, for 2 weeks under Captain Henry Towles. Re-enlisted May, 1781, for 2 months under Captain Joseph Wood. Re-enlisted Sept., 1781, for 2 months under Captain James Clark, Colonel Allcock, commander. Was engaged in the siege and surrender of Yorktown. He was born in 1754 and made his application for pension 27 Sept., 1832, from Madison County. His claim was allowed. He was alive in 1840, as given in the Revolutionary Census taken in that year. (Department of Pensions. S. File 7771.)

VIRGINIA REVOLUTIONARY SOLDIERS.

Webb, Isaac, Private, Contl. Line, 3 years' service.
Hurt, John, Chaplain, Contl. Line, 7 years' service.
White, John, Lieut., Contl. Line, 7 years' service.
Carr, Wm., Private, Contl. Line, end of war.
Womack, Ephraim, Corp., Contl. Line, 3 years' service.
Patterson, Tilman, Sgt., State Line, 3 years' service.
Harris, John, Lieut., Contl. Line, end of war.
French, Richd., Private, State Line, 3 years' service.
Seay, Reuben, Private, State Line, 3 years' service.
Bird, Reuben, Private, Contl. Line, 3 years' service.
Barrett, Wm., Capt., Contl. Line, 3 years' service.
Barrett, Cheswell, Capt., Contl. Line, 3 years' service.
Jones, Richd., Private, Contl. Line, 3 years' service.

Clark, Wm., Private, Contl. Line, 3 years' service.
Call, Richd., Major, Contl. Line, 3 years' service.
Bell, Hy., Lieut., Contl. Line, 3 years' service.
Gordon, Ambrose, Lieut., Contl. Line, 3 years' service.
Washington, Wm., Lieut-Col., Contl. Line, 7 years' service.
Jones, Thos., Private, Contl. Line, 3 years' service.
Brooke, Francis, Lieut., Contl. Line, end of war.
Robertson, Geo., Private, Contl. Line, 3 years' service.
Brooke, Jno., Lieut., Contl. Line, end of war.
Dishmon, Jas., Private, Contl. Line, end of war.
Jones, Richd., Private, Contl. Line, end of war.
Southall, Stephen, Lieut., Contl. Line, end of war.
Minns, Holman, Capt., Va. Line, June, 1776, to 22 Jan., 1784.
Minns, Callohill, Capt., Va. Line, Feb., 1776, to 22 Jan., 1784.
Buckner, Thos., Capt., Contl. Line, 7 years' service.
Middleton, Basil, Dr., Surgeon, Contl. Line, 3 years' service.
Murray, Danl., Private, Contl. Line, end of war.
Murray, Jas., Private, Contl. Line, end of war.
Salusbury, Newman, Private, Contl. Line, end of war.
Clay, Thos., Capt., State Line, 3 years' service.
Febeger, Christian, Col., Contl. Line, 7 years' service.
Thorp, Elkamah, Sgt., Contl. Line, 7 years' service.
Maddox, John, Private, Contl. Line, end of war.
Sarty, Jno., Capt., State Navy, 3 years' service.
Ashlock, Rich., Private, State Line, 3 years' service.
Crittenden, Wm., Private, State Line, 3 years' service.
Dungie, Jas., Private, State Line, 3 years' service.
Clark, Thos., Private, State Line, 3 years' service.
Wilson, Isaac, Sgt., State Line, 3 years' service.
Froman, Elijah, Private, State Artillery, 3 years, ending Feb.
    24, 1781.
Byrd, Jno., Private, State Line, 3 years' service.
Reynolds, Wm., Sgt., State Line, Feb. 1, 1777, to Feb. 1, 1781.
Selden, Saml., Lieut., Contl. Line, 3 years' service.
Clarke, Geo. R., Brig.-Genl., State Line, 3 years' service.
Edge, John, Private, Contl. Line, 3 years' service.
Brown, Jno., Sgt., Contl. Line, 3 years' service.

Fathern, Edwd., Private, Contl. Line, end of war.
Brown, Robt., Private, Contl. Line, 3 years' service.
Peyton, Jas., Private, Contl. Line, 3 years' service.
Baily, Southy, Private, Contl. Line, end of war.
Martin, Patk., Private, Contl. Line, end of war.
McDowell, Jno., Private, Contl. Line, 3 years' service.
Vaughan, Thos., Private, State Line, 3 years' service.
Dick, Alex., Major, State Line, Feb., 1776, to 27 Jan., 1784.
Jarrell, Solomon, Private, State Line, 3 years' service.
Berry, Nathl., Private, State Line, 3 years' service.
Linton, Jno., Lieut., Contl. Line, 3 years' service.
Stape, Thos., Drummer, Contl. Line, 3 years' service.
Mayfield, John, Private, Contl. Line, 3 years' service.
Mayfield, Hy., Private, Contl. Line, 3 years' service
Fitzgerald, John, Capt., Contl. Line, 7 years' service.
Mallett, Stephen, Private, Contl. Line, 3 years' service.
Jones, Churchill, Capt., Contl. Line, 3 years' service.
Dade, Francis, Capt., Contl. Line, 3 years' service.
Jackson, Wm., Private, Contl. Line, end of war.
O'Neal, Jno., Private, Contl. Line, end of war.
Moore, Wm., Private, State Line, 3 years' service.
Woolfolk, Wm., Sgt., Contl. Line, 3 years' years.
Baylor, Geo., Col., Contl. Line, 7 years' service.
Harris, Thos., Private, Contl. Line, 3 years' service.
Meredith, Wm., Capt., Contl. Line, 3 years' service.
White, Thos., Lieut., State Line, 3 years' service.
Parsons, Wm., Capt., Contl. Line, 3 years' service.
Babtiste, Jean, Private, Contl. Line, 3 years' service.
Cocke, Colin, Capt., Contl. Line, 7 years' service.
Mabon, Jas., Capt., Contl. Line, 7 years' service.
Bowman, Jas., dec'd, Private, Contl. Line, 3 years' service.
Meriwether, Jas., Lieut., State Line, 3 years' service.
Anderson, Hy., Drum Major, Contl. Line, 3 years' service.
Martin, Thos., Lieut., Contl. Line, 3 years' service.
Shepherd, David, Private, Contl. Line, 3 years' service.
Brooker, Lewis, Capt., Contl. Line, 7 years' service.
Hubbard, Elias, Private, Contl. Line, 3 years' service

Spencer, Beverly, Private, Contl. Line, 3 years' service.
Anderton, Ralph, Private, State Line, 3 years' service.
Armstrong, Adam, Private, State Line, 3 years' service.
Anderson, Wm., Private, Contl. Line, 3 years' service.
Stewart, Philip, Lieut., Contl. Line, end of war.
Rogers, John, Private, Contl. Line, 3 years' service.
Noell, Richd., Corp., Contl. Line, 3 years' service.
Taylor, Jas., Private, State Line, 3 years' service.
Davis, Wm., Private, State Line, end of war.
Grubbs, Hensley, Private, Contl. Line, 3 years' service.
Shires, Nicholas, Private, Contl. Line, 3 years' service.
Whitehend, Jno., Sailor, State Navy, 3 years' service.
Haley, Danl., Private, dec'd, Contl. Line, 3 years' service. John
Haley, representative.

NOTES AND QUERIES.

Another book on the Carters of Lancaster County is on the press. Dr. J. L. Miller, of Thomas, West Va., is the editor and compiler. The present volume concerns the descendants of Captain Thomas Carter, of "Barford," Lancaster, 1652. It gives side lights on many prominent Virginia families and is compiled from data gathered from original public and private records. From our own personal acquaintance with the author, we can assure subscribers that they will obtain a book that is reliable in what it sets forth on the family history.

We frequently receive letters from clients in which they say: "I wrote to the county clerk, but he did not reply. Can you tell me the reason?" Yes, there are several reasons. In the first place, the clerk is not a genealogist. He is paid to do the duties of his office, not to hunt pedigrees. Secondly, the queries as a rule are so garbled that it would require an expert to find out what was wanted. Finally, the old Virginia clerk with his courtly manners is fast disappearing, and the political appointee holds his office. When you find a politician who is willing to do some hard record searching for a few dollars, let us have his name. We can keep him busy ourselves.

The lax method of keeping the old records in many of the Virginia court houses will cost the historian dear before many years are past. Last May the records at Williamsburg were destroyed by fire. They were simply invaluable, as many of them were copies of wills, the originals of which had previously been destroyed by fire at the burning of Richmond. A few years ago, we compiled a small book on the wills then at Williamsburg. Only 100 copies were printed, so that the holders of copies are lucky indeed to possess one. The angel of fire is hovering over several other court houses that we wot of.

We now possess a complete MS. copy of the old Farnham Parish Register, Richmond County, births, deaths and marriages from 1672 to 1800. Clients desiring copies of extracts may have same—for a consideration.

We do not send any of our printed books on Virginia on approval. There are too many "dead beats" hunting pedigrees to suit us. We would like to hear from the D. A. R. person living in Bardstown, Ky., who purchased a book from us three years ago, and to the sending of some half dozen communications, registered letters included, she does not deign to reply. We constantly receive orders for books on approval, the would-be purchasers saying they belonged to the Colonial Dames or the D. A. R., using these organizations as a sort of Bradstreet. It makes no difference to us. The rule is cash in advance, or no book. Unreliable persons frequently belong to reliable societies. We could name quite a few.

Some ten years ago, the editor when at Amelia Court House copied the marriage bonds, some 350 in all. No more could be found, and it was supposed there were no others. The abstracts were published in Vol. IV. Va. County Records. An overhauling of the Court records was made recently and a number of packets of bonds was discovered. The result of the find is now given in the present number of the Virginia County Records, supplementing the previous bonds as published in Vol. IV.

Very few of the more recently appointed Clerks know much about the old records. Last summer, when at Warsaw, Richmond County, the Editor obtained permission to hunt through an old cupboard, which the Clerk assured us contained nothing but poll lists and papers of little value. After grubbing amongst the dust of years, we had the pleasure of unearthing some dozen packets of old marriage bonds, the earliest dating from about 1744. What we did with the find will be revealed in some future number of the Quarterly.

COLLEGE OF ARMS OF CANADA.

By Edict of King Louis XIV. in 1664: Confirmed by Royal
Commission of the Appeal of Malta of 1877.

*Under Council of the Aryan and Seigneurial Order of the
Empire in America.*

MEMORANDA.

I.

This College of Arms is the Official Court of Heraldic
Registry of America, wherein armigerous right and rank are
established and where symbols are added to the arms of those
proven under seal, that the true may be known from the false.

On account of the prevalence of fraud in American ancestry and arms, no claims of distinction thereby are accepted
anywhere unless the titles by which they are held are guaran-
teed by the Heraldic Court of the College of Arms. Costly
books on "Famous Families of America" have thus become
so worthless by the admixture of the false with the presumably genuine, that their arms and rank are unworthy of notice,
and if borne without warrant, are reckoned, in England and
America, to be warrantless through inability to obtain the seal
of the Commissioners of the Heraldic Court and the symbol
of authentication of the College of Arms.

II.

No Heraldic Court will certify to descent from armigerous
ancestry unless probative proof is given. Circumstantial evidence of bearing the same name and tradition of origin in the
same locality, with official, gentry and proprietary condition
in every generation of the family chain, are deemed worthy to

give right to bear the same arms, but with a symbol of difference to show that the right, though conceded, is circumstantial rather than documentary. In like manner, the College of Arms of Canada follows the same law by regarding the *condition* of the *First American Ancestor* as the *criterion* of his *parental condition in Europe* in the acknowledgment of traditionary and circumstantial armigerous descent and rank.

Marks of Authentication.

I.

Families of the Baronets of Nova Scotia (signed for by the Earl of Galloway in 1908; of the Seigneurs of the Empire (represented by the Duke of Veragua); of the Bannerets of Quebec (represented by the Baroness Dorchester, who founded the Dorchester decoration of the order); of the Seigneurs of Canada and Louisiana (represented by the Baron de Longueuil); of the Manorial and Titular Grantees of America (represented by the Brents of Maryland, next of kin to Lord Baltimore); of the Equestors of the Yellow Rose, Knights of the Golden Horseshoe of Virginia; of the Royal and Military Order of the Mountain Eagle, etc.—all confederated in the Aryan and Seigneurial Order—are granted a special coronet over the arms, and are eligible to the Dorchester Decoration of the Empire in the male line, family name of any of the above distinctions. So are those holding matriculation papers from the Heraldic Courts of the Seigneurial Nobility of Europe.

II.

First Ancestor to America before 1783, who used armorial seal or who was put on the list for Royal Provincial Council by order of the King, gives Consular rank to his family; to whose registered descendants of family name the Court decrees the *Consular Button* of rank, with *azure octofoil* added to recorded arms.

III.

First Ancestor to America before 1783, who was a landed proprietor and military or civil officer, gives Burgess rank with the button, and red octofoil to such arms as circumstantial evidence before the College decides.

IV.

First Ancestor to America after 1783, who was a man of property and station, and acknowledged by signed and sealed letters of an armigerous family of Europe, duly recorded there to be one of themselves, gives to his registered descendants of the name, the button of Alumnal rank, and the green octofoil of authentication is added to their registered arms.

V.

Those receiving the Button and Diploma of the Heraldic Court of the College of Arms are armigers of the same, ranked with the Armigerous Nobility of Europe by international treaties of comity. Armigers of 16 quarterings are admitted to the Seigneurial Order and Decoration.

Court Dress.

The Seigneurial Order has its own Dress and Decoration of the Empire. The Armigers wear the conventional black dress, but with gilt buttons and epaulettes; dress sword; blue, red or green sash, rosette and button of Consular, Burgess or Alumnal Degree; black felt hat with gilt band; blue, red or green feather.

SOME PROVINCIAL FAMILIES OF NEW YORK RANKED IN THE
NOBLESSE OF CANADA AS BANNERETS OF QUEBEC
IN THE ARCHIVES OF THE COLLEGE OF ARMS
OF CANADA.

COMPILED BY THE HERALD-MARSHAL

Among the early members of the various orders which
were made nobilities on the American Continent are enumer-
ated the Caciques and Landgraves of the Carolinas, the Lords-
Patroons of New Netherland and New York, the Seigneurs
of Canada and Louisiana, the Lords of the Maryland and
South Carolina Manours, the Baronets of Nova Scotia, the
Bannerets of Quebec, the Equestors of the Yellow Rose, etc.

The State of New York and adjoining country were rich
in these Bannerets of Quebec. They as a body were raised to
the rank of a nobility—a fact not known generally—and it
gives additional interest in the statement to the great number
living in New York who are descended from these eminent
personages. At the present time, the English administration
in Canada, under tutelage of that in England, wishes the fact
to be forgotten that the Loyalists were made a nobility, or to
be regarded as a "fiction" of the law to be observed in the
non-observance. But the royal ordinance remains, and the
administration has never dared to abrogate it. The lack of
faith in these observances of obligations, especially under the
House of Hanover, was great enough to have caused the
American revolt against the infringement of Colonial charters
and constitutions in 1775 and the war for independence in
1776, and has been great enough ever since to wish to undo the
Loyalist Act of 1789 creating the Loyalists a nobility, which
was done in a moment of hasty enthusiasm. This Act passed
at Quebec under signature of the Governor-General Guy
Carleton, Lord Dorchester, and that of his council of the Seigneurs of the Country and his other advising officers declared it
to be the intention to "put a mark of honor on those families
that joined the Royal Standard in America in the late war"
(1776-83). The reason for this is declared in the Act to be
that they should be distinguished from other colonists in the

country on account of their noble and distinguished services. It is but just to say that this Loyalist Act making of those "who joined the Royal Standard" a nobility was done by themselves and their friends the Seigneurs of Canada when they were in possession of the government and no administration since has dared undo the act. Moreover, it was acknowledged —with bad grace, no doubt—by the King George III. But the English themselves failed to see in this loyalty and devotion any other attribute than a servile obedience to the government. They could not—much less their stupid and bull-headed leaders —appreciate the fact that the noblest of these so-called Loyalists were loyal to their colonial charters, against whose infringements most of them had stood—even against the infringements by the British parliament itself up to 1778, and after that time, with the parliament that had abrogated the infringements and against the revolutionists who were altering the colonial charters which they were claiming to defend, and establishing a democracy contrary to their previous pledges and engagements with the people of the colonies themselves.

Had these Loyalists, loyal as they were to the colonies to which they belonged and to the charters of those colonies, instead of joining with the Crown and Parliament in 1778-83, united among themselves to form a party in the colonies for independence along the line of the meaning of the original charters, it can not be doubted but that their strength and influence would have caused a better form of government to have been chosen than the one at present in the United States.

A brief sketch of a few of these loyalists will show their importance. And their descendants, by the Loyalist Act of 1789, have the rights of precedence as a nobility in Canada.

Theophilact Bache, vice-president of the New York Chamber of Commerce in 1782, whose brother Richard married Sarah, daughter of Dr. Benj Franklin, was true to the Crown. While the colonies were making a constitutional struggle for their rights, he was with Lewis and Jay, a member of the committee of correspondence. But when they decided to rebel and form a republic, he stood staunchly for his royalist principles. At one time the revolutionists held him a prisoner in New Jersey. His kindness even to adversaries in that war was "worthy of respect." He died in New York in 1807. *The Barclays* of New York are mentioned as "Americans of royal descent. The bluest blood of New York Society is said to be derived mostly from Barclay affiliation. Rev. Dr. Henry Barclay was rector of Trinity in 1765. His daughter Nancy married Col. Beverly Robinson, a loyalist and father of Sir Frederic Robinson, of Toronto. His son, Thomas Barclay, was a major under Sir Henry Clinton in 1777, who left the country with the British, but returned and died in New York in 1830. He was father of Col. De Lancey Barclay, who distinguished himself at Waterloo and was A. D. C. to King George IV.

Five of the most prominent members of the Bayard family that claim to trace their ancestry to the same source as that from which arose the great chevalier Du Terrail de Bayard, "sans peur et sans reproche," were loyalists. In 1782 John Bayard was lieutenant-colonel of the King's Orange (N. Y.) Rangers. Robert was royal judge in admiralty in 1782 and his estates were confiscated by the republicans. Samuel was a signer to the crown in 1774 and in 1782 was major of the King's Orange Rangers, and his son Samuel was deputy secretary for the Crown in 1782. Samuel Vetch Bayard was a Crown officer and settled in New Brunswick. Col. William Bayard, of North River, had his property confiscated because of his royalist principles.

Fourteen of the landed proprietors of the Brickerhoff name of Queen's Co. testified to their unalterable allegiance to royalty in 1776. Few in 1776 could exceed the fame of the Coldens, chief of whom was Cadwaller Colden, Surveyor-General of the colony, and member of the King's council. He was lieutenant-governor in 1761. His son David, who married Ann, daughter of John Willett, of Flushing, had his property taken by the democrats and went to England. He was father of Cadweller D. Colden, one of the most eminent of New York lawyers, who, with de Witt Clinton, promoted the Erie Canal. He died in Jersey City in 1834. John, another of the Coldens, was a loyalist captain of New Jersey Volunteers, and his relative, Thomas Colden, was captain in the Pennsylvania Loyalist regiment.

Thirteen of the Cornells of Queen's Co. acknowledged allegiance to the Crown in opposition to the democrats in 1776, from one of whom is descended the founder of Cornell University.

In 1775, John Cruger was President of the New York assembly and that year addressed a letter to Gen. Gage on the threatened uprising of the democracy. His relative, John Harris Cruger, who married a daughter of Col. de Lancey, was a royal counsellor. His property was confiscated for his loyalty.

If any colonial family deserve the term of "Noble" it is that of de Lancey. James de Lancey of New York was colonel of a loyalist regiment, and fought for the Crown, settled in Nova Scotia and was a member of the council of that colony. His cousin, James de Lancey, an officer of Oliver de Lancey's loyalist regiment, was afterwards collector of His Majesty's Customs at New Providence. Oliver de Lancey whose brother James was at one time chief-justice and Lieut.-Gov. of New York and whose father was of the French noblesse, became a general on the side of the Crown. He went to England at the close of the war and was a member of parliament. His daughter married Sir Wm. Draper. His son Oliver, Jr., was Adj.-Gen. in the British Army. His cousin, Stephen, was a loyalist colonel and afterwards chief-justice of the Bahamas. His wife was a daughter of Dr. Barclay of New York, and their son was an A. D. C. to Lord Wellington at Waterloo.

The de Peysters have continued at the head of affairs. Their descent from the counts de Tourhaute in the Netherlands and the claim that family have on that title, rank them with the colonial nobility. Capt. Abram de Peyster was second in command of the King's troops at the Battle of King's

Mountain in 1780. His life was saved in that battle by a gold doubloon in his pocket shielding him from a republican bullet. He went to St. John in 1783 and was colonel of the New Brunswick militia and treasurer of that province. His relative, Capt. Frederic de Peyster, of the New York loyalists went also to St. John where he received a grant of land and was a magistrate. He returned to New York where he died in 1828. From him was descended the late Frederic de Peyster, LL.D., President of the New York Historical Society and father of the late Gen. John Watts de Peyster, the noted author on military topics who was also a member of the United Empire Loyalist Association of Canada.

At the house of James Graham, of Ulster County, a number of the adherents of King George met in 1775 and raised a royal standard on a staff seventy feet high. On the staff was the following inscription: "In testimony of our unshaken loyalty and incorruptible fidelity to the best of kings: of our inviolable attachment to the parent state and to the British constitution: of our abhorrence...of a republican government ...seditious meeting and execrable mobs...this stand is erected by a number of His Majesty's most faithful subjects in Ulster County on the 10th February, in the 15th year of the reign of our most excellent sovereign, King George III." This family of Graham claim descent from a younger son of the Duke of Montrose.

The Harpers of Queen's Co. who suffered for their loyalty were represented by James and Thomas. From this family are descended the Harper brothers who have established one of the greatest publishing houses in the World.

In 1782, Francis Kearney was major in the Pennsylvania loyalist regiment and Michael Kearney was searcher in the superintendent's department of New York under the Crown. Gen. Philip Kearney came of this stock and was related to the de Peysters.

Twenty-two of the Lawrences of Queen's were royalist associates from 1776 to 1779. One of them was a colonel and another was a captain under the Crown. A large estate in

England was in the property of this family and some sort of connection existed between them and the Hydes, Earls of Clarendon.

There were more of the great Livingston family for royalty than for republicanism in 1776. Their descent from a noble Scottish house; their possession of the manour of Livingston on the Hudson; their connection with persons and things high and ennobling must have had their due weight. Henry Livingston was an officer of royalist cavalry in South Carolina in 1782. John, Jr., was seized by the republicans at Jamaica, N. Y., in 1776 for his royalist principles and made a prisoner. Gilbert was a captain in the American Loyalist Legion. John was a captain in the King's American Regiment and Philip was a Crown officer in 1780 at New York.

Roger Morris, one of the manorial family of that name, whose wife was a daughter of Frederic Philipse, had served in the French war on staff of Gen. Braddock. In 1775 he was a royal counsellor. He was a colonel under the Crown. His large estate in New York was not entirely confiscated, for his son, Capt. Henry Gage Morris, R. N., in 1809 in behalf of his two sisters and himself sold their revisionary interest to John Jacob Astor for £20,000 sterling, for which Mr. Astor received from the state of New York $500,000 in 1828. Another son was Capt. Amherst Morris, so named for his god-father Lord Amherst. It is said that Washington came a-courting Mrs. Morris when she was Miss Philipse but he was not deemed an eligible *parti.*

Among the leading members of the Ogdens who were true to the Crown in 1776, were the Hon. Benjamin Ogden of Westchester Co.; Isaac, barrister at New York; Jonathan of whom it was written that he was "Among the faithful and intrepid band of loyalists, who for their unshaken attachment to the throne and constitution of Great Britain suffered much in their early days." Peter, who was secretary of the New York Police Department in 1782; the Hon. Robert, at one time President of the New Jersey Assembly and last the most illustrious of all, the Hon. David Ogden, Royal Coun-

sellor, judge of the N. J. Supreme Court and member of the
N. J. Loyalist Society of 1779. He planned the outline of a
government for America. It was as follows: "That the right
of taxation of America by the British Parliament be given up:
that the colonies be restored to their former constitutions; that
each colony have a governor and council appointed by the
Crown and a house of representatives elected by the free-
holders: that an American parliament be established, to con-
sist of a Lord-Lieutenant, Barons (to be created for the purpose by His Majesty): a house of commons to be elected
by the assemblies of the various colonies: which parliament to
be styled 'The Lord Lieutenant, the Lords and Commons of
the British Colonies of North America.' "

The Philipses were among the founders of New York.
Frederic Philipse came from Holland in 1658, bringing money,
plate and jewels and the patents of two patroon-lordships
on the Hudson, called Philipsbourg and Fredericksbourg. The
former contained 150 square miles, the latter 240. He owned
many houses in the city; he laid out lots and streets and built
a town residence. His four children were Frederic, Philip,
Susan married to Col. Beverly Robinson and Mary married
to Col. Roger Morris. The son Frederic was a colonel and a
member of the provincial assembly. In 1775 he attended a
republican meeting only to declare that his purpose in coming
was "To protest against its illegal and unconstitutional pro-
ceedings." He retired to England later on rather than see a
republic established. His nephews and nieces inherited the
property.

The Hon. John Rapalje of New York, was a royal signer
in 1775 as well as sixteen others of the name living in Queen's
Co.

Jacob Schureman was so inimical to republican institutions that he left New York in 1783 and settled in Prince Edward's Island. From him is descended Mr. Schureman of the
Philippine Commission. The family claim the title of baron
von Schureman, deriving it from a German ancestor.

The Hon. Peter Tenbroeck was a royal signer in 1775: he was magistrate of Tryon, Montgomery Co., N. Y.

Richard Townsend, of North Hempstead was a distinguished royalist in 1782. Twenty-two of the name in Queen's testified their allegiance to Lord Howe in 1776. John, magistrate at Oyster Bay and Benj., an ensign of the New York Loyalist Regiment, completes this family's list.

Of the old Knickerbocker Vans, there were Joost Van Brunt of Jamaica; the leader of the Van Buskirks among them, Col. Abram, who commanded the N. Y. Loyalist Regiment; Anthony Van Dam; James Van Deusen; Lieut. Wm. Van Dumont; Col. Gabriel de Veber of the Prince of Wales' American Regiment; Gabriel and Capt. Wm. Van Horn and thirteen Van Nostrands of Queen's Co. The name of Van Courtlandt, replete with the glories of colonial belongings and manorial dignities stands prominently forth. Hon. Philip Van Courtlandt of Westchester, was a major in the N. Y. Loyalist Regiment in 1782. One of his daughters married Sir Edward Buller, R. N., and another, Capt. Evans, of the British Army. One of the sons, Philip, Jr., was an ensign in his father's regiment. The home of the race, Courtlandt Manour, is one of the most famous in America, and is the only patroonate in possession of the original family.

The Hon. Peter Van Shaack of Kinderhook, was obliged to seek shelter in England on account of his royalist views. He returned to New York after 1783 and became a leading member of the legal profession. He died in New York in 1832, and an account of his life was published by his son.

Nearly all of the Watts were royalists. They were connected with the Earls of Cassilis in Scotland. The Hon. John Watts, Royal Counsellor of N. Y., had a daughter married to Sir John Johnson, and his son served in the loyalist corps raised by Sir John. His relatives, George and George, Jr., of Queen's, were royal signers in 1776.

It is natural that the Zabriskies should have been on the same side since they claim descent from the Kings of Poland. The most prominent of them in 1776 was Hon.

John Zabriskie, magistrate, whose estate in New Jersey was taken by the republican congress and given to Baron von Steuben in reward for services. Peter Zabriskie was on the loyalist correspondence committee in 1774.

SOME LOYALISTS ENTITLED BY THE ACT OF 1789 TO RANK AS BANNERETS OF QUEBEC, IN REGISTERS OF COLLEGE OF ARMS OF CANADA.

COMPILED BY THE REGISTRAR-GENERAL.

Addison, Rev. H., of Maryland. Born ——; died ——. In 1783 was in New York. In Loyalist tract, published in London, 1784, was cited as a gentleman of large property.

Addison, Daniel Delaney, of Maryland. Born, 1758; died, 1808. Entered the Maryland Loyalists in 1776. Was a captain in 1782, and major at the peace. Died in London.

Agnew, John, Rev., of Virginia. Born, 1727; died, 1812. Rector established church parish, Suffolk, Va.; Chaplain Queen's Rangers. Died in Frederickton, New Brunswick.

Agnew, Stair, of Virginia. Born, 1754; died, 1821. Son of Rev. John Agnew, of Virginia. Captain Queen's Rangers. After the peace, settled in Frederickton, New Brunswick.

Aikman, Alexander. Born, 1755, in Scotland; settled in South Carolina. Died in 1838 in Prospect Pen, St. Andrews. Was printer to House of Assembly and to the King.

Allen, William. Born, ——; died, 1780, in England. Was chief-justice of Pennsylvania, until the approach of the revolution, when he went to England.

Allen, William, of Pennsylvania. Born, ——; died, ——. Son of Chief-Justice Allen. In 1778 raised a corps called Pennsylvania Loyalists, and was commanding officer. In 1783 was one of the grantees of St. John, New Brunswick.

Allen, Andrew, of Pennsylvania. Born, 1750; died, 1825.
Son of Chief-Justice Allen. Was under protection of
Gen. Howe in 1776. After the peace, settled in London
and died there.

Allen, Isaac, of Trenton, New Jersey. Born, 1741; died,
1806. Was in military service of the Crown. Lieutenant-
colonel 2d Battalion, New Jersey Volunteers. After
the peace, settled in St. John, New Brunswick. Was one
of the grantees of that city.

Allen, Jolly, of Boston. Born, ——; died, 1782. Left Boston in 1776 with the Royal Army. Died in England.

Allison, Edward, of Long Island, N. Y. Born,——; died,
——. Captain in De Lancy's 3d Battalion. At the peace,
settled in New Brunswick.

Althouse, John, of New York. Born, ——; died, ——. In
1782 was captain in the New York Volunteers. At the
peace settled in St. John, New Brunswick, and was one
of the grantees of that city.

Ambrose, Michael, of New York. Born, ——; died, ——.
In 1782 was a Lieutenant in the Prince of Wales' American Volunteers. At the peace settled in New Brunswick,
and died at St. Martin's.

Anderson, Samuel, of New York. Born, 1735; died, 1836.
At the beginning of the revolution entered the service
of the Crown, and was Captain under Sir John Johnson.
In 1783 settled near Cornwall, Canada, and died there.

Anderson, William, of West Chester, N. Y. Born, ——; died,
——. At the peace settled in Shelburne, Nova Scotia,
then in St. John, New Brunswick, and was one of the
grantees of that city.

Anderson, Peter, of New York. Born, 1783; died, 1828.
Was a Loyalist Associate. At the peace settled in St.
John, New Brunswick, and was one of the grantees of
that city.

Anderson, Joseph, of New York. Born, 1760; died, 1853.
Lieutenant in the King's regiment of New York. He was

known as "one of the last survivors of the United Empire Loyalists."

Anderson, James, of Boston, Mass. Born, ——; died, ——. Was Captain of the Scotch Co. at Boston, Mass. Died in Canada.

Andrews, Samuel, of North Carolina. Born, ——; died, ——. Was Major in the Loyalist militia. In 1781 he raised a company and joined Lord Cornwallis. In 1785 he settled in Shelburne, Canada.

Ansley, Ozias, of New Jersey. Born, 1753; died, 1828. Was Ensign in the 1st Battalion New Jersey Volunteers and Adjutant of the corps. At the peace settled in New Brunswick, later returned to Staten Island, N. Y., where he died.

Atkins, Charles, of Charleston, South Carolina. Born, ——; died, —— Received a military commission, and in 1782 was an officer in the volunteers. At the peace, settled in London, where he died.

Anderson, Samuel, of Maryland. Born, ——; died, ——. Was Captain of the King's Rangers.

Alstyn, P. Van, of New York. Born, ——; died, ——. In 1775 was magistrate at Kinderhook. In 1780 was Captain in Cuyler's Corps stationed on Long Island.

Allicock, Charles John, of South Carolina. Born, ——; died, ——. In 1782 was a Lieutenant in the South Carolina Cavalry.

Anderson, John, of South Carolina. Born, ——; died, ——. Was Captain of the King's Rangers.

COLLEGE OF ARMS OF CANADA.

In Washington, on the evening of Nov. 16, there was a meeting of the Imperial Order of the Yellow Rose, being the organized descendants of those families entitled to the Consular, Burgess and Alumnal registry of the College of Arms of Canada, but who in addition trace through some line to Royal ancestry. This order is under the presidency, as "Chief Regent,' of Dr. J. G. B. Bulloch, Pursuyvant of the College of Arms of Canada, who was present and conducted the meeting. The Hon. Thomas Scott Forsyth, Registrar-General of the College of Arms of Canada, was the guest of the evening.

At the meeting was announced the opening of the Seigneurial Court and Council to take place at Montreal, Sept. 10-15, 1912, at which all families capable of registering in the manorial, titular, consular, burgess or alumnal rank of the College of Arms of Canada are entitled to be represented in the imperial pageantry of that occasion. For that purpose committees are being formed of ladies and gentlemen in the various states under the leadership of Dr. Bulloch, 2122 P St., N. W., Washington, D. C.

Each family after registering its rank and pedigree in the College of Arms of Canada and receiving its diploma and certificate prepares its own banner to be borne in the pageantry. The pole of the banner is 6 feet long, covered with gilt paper. The cross-piece is 2 feet long, covered the same, and fastened to the pole 6 inches from the top. The cloth on which the family arms is painted is 2 feet square and the family shield is 1 foot wide by 1½ feet deep. The color of the cloth is the same as the most prominent object in the family shield. The octofoil of rank is painted at the base of the family shield and again in a 6 square inch space at the right corner of the banner itself.

In the march past the throne in the great edifice in Montreal where this court is held, the members of each family present march with their own banner in line to be presented and then to their seats reserved for them. The men dress according to the rule published in last issue and the women and children according to choice, but with their appropriate sashes, etc.

The imperial order of programme is led by the Bearer of the Sword of State; then comes the Bearer of the Sceptre of Dominion; then the Imperial Standard of Charles V of 1540. Under a canopy on a litter borne by four beautiful daughters of the Seigneurs repose the Crown of Empire with the Scroll of Laws tied with yellow, blue, red and green ribbons. The military orchestra play the Imperial March. Then follow the Seigneurial, armorial, titular, consular, burgess and alumnal families with their banners. When they arrive at their places the Crown, Sceptre and Scroll are deposited at the top of the throne. The military salute of swords is given. The Imperial Hymn, "God Save the Emperor," is chanted in Latin, while incense is burnt, and the interesting ceremonies begin. This will be the most illustrious assemblage ever held in America, since it will be that of the families that founded the feudal and splendid civilization of Europe in America under the Crown and according to the institutions of the ancient empire.

INDEX TO VOL. IX

Early Settlers in Virginia, 13.

Family History, Hill, 112, Lyon, 32, 109.

Henrico County Abstracts, 18, 59.

Land Grants, Dinwiddie, 48; Gloucester, 37, Halifax 103; King George, 99; Rappahannock, 1; Richmond, 7.

Marriage Bonds, Amelia 119; Caroline, 12; Northampton, 115; Orange, 55; Pittsylvania, 121.

i

Wills and Administrations.

Canadian Section.

www.ingramcontent.com/pod-product-compliance
Lightning Source LLC
Chambersburg PA
CBHW061742270326
41928CB00011B/2336